Practice Planners

Arthur E. Jongsma, Jr., Series Editor

W9-AEQ-496

Helping therapists help their clients...

Treatment Planners cover all the necessary elements for developing formal treatment plans, including detailed problem definitions, long-term goals, short-term objectives, therapeutic interventions, and DSM-IV™ diagnoses.

- ❏ The Complete Adult Psychotherapy Treatment Planner, Third Edition ....0-471-27113-6 / $49.95
- ❏ The Child Psychotherapy Treatment Planner, Third Edition............................0-471-27050-4 / $49.95
- ❏ The Adolescent Psychotherapy Treatment Planner, Third Edition ....0-471-27049-0 / $49.95
- ❏ The Addiction Treatment Planner, Second Edition ....0-471-41814-5 / $49.95
- ❏ The Couples Psychotherapy Treatment Planner ....0-471-24711-1 / $49.95
- ❏ The Group Therapy Treatment Planner ....0-471-25469-X / $49.95
- ❏ The Family Therapy Treatment Planner ....0-471-34768-X / $49.95
- ❏ The Older Adult Psychotherapy Treatment Planner ....0-471-29574-4 / $49.95
- ❏ The Employee Assistance (EAP) Treatment Planner ....0-471-24709-X / $49.95
- ❏ The Gay and Lesbian Psychotherapy Treatment Planner ....0-471-35080-X / $49.95
- ❏ The Crisis Counseling and Traumatic Events Treatment Planner ....0-471-39587-0 / $49.95
- ❏ The Social Work and Human Services Treatment Planner ....0-471-37741-4 / $49.95
- ❏ The Continuum of Care Treatment Planner ....0-471-19568-5 / $49.95
- ❏ The Behavioral Medicine Treatment Planner...0-471-31923-6 / $49.95
- ❏ The Mental Retardation and Developmental Disability Treatment Planner ....0-471-38253-1 / $49.95
- ❏ The Special Education Treatment Planner..0-471-38872-6 / $49.95
- ❏ The Severe and Persistent Mental Illness Treatment Planner.......................0-471-35945-9 / $49.95
- ❏ The Personality Disorders Treatment Planner ....0-471-39403-3 / $49.95
- ❏ The Rehabilitation Psychology Treatment Planner ....0-471-35178-4 / $49.95
- ❏ The Pastoral Counseling Treatment Planner...0-471-25416-9 / $49.95
- ❏ The Juvenile Justice and Residential Care Treatment Planner ....0-471-43320-9 / $49.95
- ❏ The School Counseling and School Social Work Treatment Planner ....0-471-08496-4 / $49.95
- ❏ The Psychopharmacology Treatment Planner ....0-471-43322-5 / $49.95
- ❏ The Probation and Parole Treatment Planner...0-471-20244-4 / $49.95
- ❏ The Suicide and Homicide Risk Assessment
  and Prevention Treatment Planner ....0-471-46631-X / $49.95
- ❏ The Speech-Language Pathology Treatment Planner.......................................0-471-27504-2 / $49.95
- ❏ The College Student Counseling Treatment Planner ....0-471-46708-1 / $49.95
- ❏ The Parenting Skills Treatment Planner ....0-471-48183-1 / $49.95
- ❏ The Early Childhood Treatment Planner ....0-471-65962-2 / $49.95

The **Complete Treatment and Homework Planners** series of books combines our bestselling *Treatment Planners* and *Homework Planners* into one easy-to-use, all-in-one resource for mental health professionals treating clients suffering from the most commonly diagnosed disorders.

- ❏ The Complete Depression Treatment and Homework Planner.....................0-471-64515-X / $39.95
- ❏ The Complete Anxiety Treatment and Homework Planner ....0-471-64548-6 / $39.95

WILEY

Practice*Planners*®

Homework Planners feature dozens of behaviorally based, ready-to-use assignments that are designed for use between sessions, as well as a disk (Microsoft Word) containing all of the assignments—allowing you to customize them to suit your unique client needs.

Progress Notes Planners contain complete prewritten progress notes for each presenting problem in the companion Treatment Planners.

Client Education Handout Planners contain elegantly designed handouts that can be printed out from the enclosed CD-ROM and provide information on a wide range of psychological and emotional disorders and life skills issues. Use as patient literature, handouts at presentations, and aids for promoting your mental health practice.

Name_____

Affiliation_____

Address_____

City/State/Zip_____

Phone/Fax_____

E-mail_____

❑ Check enclosed ❑ Visa ❑ MasterCard ❑ American Express

Card #_____

Expiration Date _____

Signature _____

Add $6 shipping for first book, $1 for each additional book. Please add your local sales tax to all orders. Prices subject to change without notice.

To order by phone in the US:
Call toll free 1-877-762-2974

Fax: 1-800-597-3299

Online: www.practiceplanners.wiley.com

Mail this order form to:
John Wiley & Sons, Attn: J. Knott,
111 River Street, Hoboken, NJ 07030

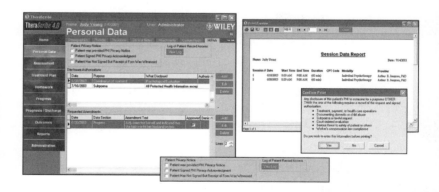

Need Help Getting Started?

Getting Started in Personal and Executive Coaching offers a go-to reference designed to help build, manage, and sustain a thriving coaching practice. Packed with hundreds of proven strategies and techniques, this nuts-and-bolts guide covers all aspects of the coaching business with step-by-step instructions and real-world illustrations that prepare you for every phase of starting your own coaching business.

This single, reliable book offers straightforward advice and tools for running a successful practice, including:

- Seven secrets of highly successful coaches
- Fifteen strategies for landing paying clients
- Ten marketing mistakes to avoid
- Sample business and marketing plans
- Worksheets for setting rates and managing revenue

Getting Started in Personal and Executive Coaching
Stephen G. Fairley and Chris E. Stout
ISBN 0-471-42624-5
Paper • $24.95 • 356pp • December 2003

Getting Started in Private Practice provides all the information you need to confidently start and grow your own mental health practice. This book breaks down the ingredients of practice into more manageable and achievable components and will teach you the skills you need to avoid making costly mistakes. Containing dozens of tools that you can use to achieve your goals, this book has specific information that can be applied to your business today, worksheets that will help you calculate the true costs of various expenditures and activities, checklists that might save you from disaster, and lists of resources to investigate. Includes:

- Forms and examples of various practice aspects
- Step-by-step advice on writing a business plan and marketing your business
- Suggestions and ideas intended to help you get your creative juices flowing
- Practical and simple formulas to help calculate rates, revenues, and Return on Investment
- Comprehensive information on licensing procedures and risk management

Getting Started in Private Practice
Chris E. Stout and Laurie Cope Grand
ISBN 0-471-42623-7
Paper • $24.95 • 304 pp. • October 2004

WILEY
Now you know.
wiley.com

The Couples Psychotherapy Treatment Planner

K. Daniel O'Leary

Richard E. Heyman

Arthur E. Jongsma, Jr.

JOHN WILEY & SONS, INC.

New York • Chichester • Weinheim • Brisbane • Singapore • Toronto

This publication is designed to provide accurate and authoritative
information in regard to the subject matter covered. It is sold with
the understanding that the publisher is not engaged in rendering
professional services. If legal, accounting, medical, psychological or
any other expert assistance is required, the services of a competent
professional person should be sought.

Library of Congress Cataloging-in-Publication Data

O'Leary, K. Daniel, 1940–
    The couples psychotherapy treatment planner / K. Daniel O'Leary,
  Richard E. Heyman, Arthur E. Jongsma, Jr.
      p.   cm.
    Includes bibliographical references and index.
      ISBN 0-471-24711-1 (pbk. : alk. paper). — ISBN 0-471-24710-3 (paper/disk)
      1. Marital psychotherapy.   2. Marital conflict—Treatment—Planning.
  I. Heyman, Richard E., 1964–   II. Jongsma, Arthur E., 1943–
  III. Title.
  RC488.5.0395   1998
  616.89'156—dc21   98-15935
                                                                CIP

Printed in the United States of America.

10 9 8 7

CONTENTS

PREFACE

The authors' purpose in writing *The Couples Psychotherapy Treatment Planner* is to facilitate the analysis and treatment of those problems most commonly encountered by therapists who deal with relationships between couples. Relationship problems figure significantly in approximately 40 percent of all cases treated at mental health clinics (Gurin, Veroff, and Feld, 1960; Veroff, Kulka, and Douvan, 1981). Of all the stressful situations that people face in life, divorce and marital problems rank second and third, respectively—exceeded only by the trauma accompanying the death of a spouse or close relative (Holmes and Rahe, 1967). Relationship problems dramatically elevate the risk for clinical depression (Weissman, 1987; O'Leary, Christian, and Mendell, 1994; Whisman & Bruce, 1998), and they are overwhelmingly cited as the most common reasons for attempted suicides.

Couple relationship problems are not only significant in their own right (the U.S. divorce rate currently hovers at around 50 percent), but they also impact on a host of individual problems. Therapists who treat either adult or childhood problems inevitably encounter relationship and marital problems in many of their clinical diagnoses. This *Planner*, therefore, will be useful not only to those specializing in couple relationships but also to therapists dealing even peripherally with relationships.

In some instances, decreases in relationship strife can certainly lead to lessening of individual or family problems. For example, when relationship problems are perceived as the cause of a woman's depression, resolution or reduction of the relationship problems will be accompanied by significant decreases in the depression (Beach, Sandeen, and O'Leary, 1990). Similarly, if parents are experiencing relationship problems (e.g., arguments over child-rearing), individual problems being experienced by their children are likely to lessen once the adults' problems are resolved (Dodds, Schwartz, and Saunders, 1987; Pfiffner Jouriles, Brown, Etscheid, and Kelly, 1990). When patients present dual diagnoses, it is important to know as much as possible about the individual or childhood problem (psychopathology) and its treatment. Such knowledge enhances the ability of a therapist to deal with both the relationship problem and the individual or family problem.

This *Planner* defines many treatment goals and many alternative treatment procedures for reaching those particular goals. It must be emphasized however, that a treatment planner is not a substitute for clinical training or professional judgment; implementation of particular treatment goals will depend upon the nuances of each individual case.

On a personal note, this collaboration between three authors was a marvel of the electronic age. Dan O'Leary and Rick Heyman, both in Stony Brook, New York, have never physically met Art Jongsma, who lives in Grand Rapids, Michigan. Chapter manuscripts were repeatedly e-mailed back and forth through their various iterations. We all look forward to someday having dinner together, accompanied by our amiable and able editor at John Wiley & Sons, Kelly Franklin. We'd like to thank our spouses (Susan O'Leary, Maria Vanoni, and Judy Jongsma) and our families, who patiently supported us through the writing of this book, including times when we interrupted holidays and vacations to transmit chapters and corrections from various far-flung locations.

K. Daniel O'Leary
Richard E. Heyman
Arthur E. Jongsma, Jr.

INTRODUCTION

Formalized treatment planning, which began in the medical sector in the 1960s, has become an integral component of mental health service delivery in the 1990s. To meet the standards of the Joint Commission on Accreditation of Healthcare Organizations (JCAHO), and to help clients qualify for third-party reimbursement, treatment plans must be specific as to problem definitions and interventions, individualized to meet the clients' needs and goals, and measurable in terms of setting milestones that can be used to chart their progress.

Although treatment plans are now a necessity, many clinicians lack formal training in their development of such documentation. The difficulties of quickly generating accurate, customized plans are compounded by the need to acknowledge the couples treatment modality while enabling the clients to qualify for reimbursement under insurance plans more commonly geared to individual treatment. The purpose of this book, therefore, is to clarify, simplify, improve, and accelerate the couples psychotherapy treatment planning process.

TREATMENT PLAN UTILITY

Detailed measurable, written treatment plans can benefit not only the clients but also the therapist, the treatment team, the insurance community, the treatment agency, and even the overall mental health profession. The clients are served by a written plan because it clearly delineates the issues that are the focus of their treatment. It is very easy for both the therapist and the clients to lose sight of the issues that initially brought them into treatment. The treatment plan is a guide that structures the focus of the therapeutic contract. Because issues can change as treatment progresses, the treatment plan must be viewed as a dynamic document, to be updated to reflect major changes of problem, definition, goal, objective, or intervention as they occur.

While recognizing that the plan may evolve throughout treatment, it nevertheless remains important to settle on specific treatment goals at the outset. Behaviorally-based, measurable objectives clearly focus the treatment endeavor, and provide a means of measuring treatment outcome. Clear objectives also allow the clients to channel their efforts into specific changes leading to the long-term goal of problem resolution.

Therapists are aided by treatment plans because they are forced to think analytically and critically about which interventions are best suited for a particular client or couple. In multiprovider settings, treatment plans not only help to clarify objectives but also serve the important function of delineating which clinician is responsible for what intervention. By providing a common language, *The Couples Psychotherapy Treatment Planner* can facilitate consistent and clear communication between members of the treatment team and with the clients.

Good communication improves the quality of care and mitigates risk to the therapist. Malpractice suits are increasing in frequency, and insurance premiums are soaring. The first line of defense against allegations is a complete clinical record detailing the treatment process. A written, customized, formal treatment plan that has been reviewed and signed by the clients, coupled with contemporaneous, problem-oriented progress notes, is a powerful defense against false claims.

Every treatment agency or institution is constantly looking for ways to increase the quality and uniformity of the documentation in the clinical record. The demand for accountability from third-party payers and health maintenance organizations (HMOs) is partially satisfied by adding a standardized, written treatment plan and complete progress notes to each client's file. Such a plan (with problem definitions, goals, objectives, and interventions) enhances that uniformity of documentation and offers a means of improving care.

Finally, the psychotherapy profession as a whole stands to benefit from the use of more precise, measurable objectives to evaluate success in mental health treatment. With the advent of detailed treatment plans, outcome data can be more easily collected for interventions that are effective in achieving specific goals.

HOW TO DEVELOP A TREATMENT PLAN

The process of developing a treatment plan involves a logical series of steps that build on one another. The foundation of any effective treatment plan is the data gathered in a thorough biopsychosocial assessment. As the clients present themselves for treatment, the therapist must listen sensitively to discern where their struggles lie—in terms of family-of-origin issues, current stressors, emotional status concerns, social network pressures, physical health problems, coping skills, interpersonal conflicts, and so on. Assessment data may be gathered from such diverse sources as social histories, physical exams, clinical interviews, psychological tests, and genograms. The integration of this data by the therapist or the multidisciplinary treatment team is critical for understanding the clients' individual issues, and their dynamics as a couple. Once the assessment is complete, use the following six steps to develop a treatment plan.

Step One: Problem Selection

This *Couples Psychotherapy Treatment Planner* offers treatment plan components for 31 problems most commonly affecting couples. Although the clients may discuss a variety of issues during the assessment, the clinician must ferret out the most significant problems on which to focus the treatment process. Usually a *primary* problem (e.g., infidelity) will surface, and *secondary* problems (e.g., jealousy) may also be evident. Some *other* problems may have to be set aside as not urgent enough to require immediate treatment. An effective treatment plan can only deal with a few selected problems, or treatment will lose its direction.

In choosing which problems to focus on, it is important to note both those problems that are most acute or disruptive to the clients' functioning independently or as a couple and those concerns that are personally most important to the clients. The clients' motivation to participate in and cooperate with the treatment process depends, to some extent, on the degree to which treatment addresses their greatest needs.

Step Two: Problem Definition

Each pair of clients reveals with unique nuances how a problem behaviorally manifests itself in their daily lives together. Therefore, each problem selected for treatment focus requires a definition specific to the particular clients. The symptom pattern should be associated with diagnostic criteria and codes such as those found in the *Diagnostic and Statistical Manual* (DSM) or the *International Classification of Diseases*. *The Couples Psychotherapy Treatment Planner*, following the pattern established by DSM-IV, offers an array of behaviorally specific problem definition statements. Each of the 31 presenting problems has several behavioral symptoms from which to choose. These prewritten definitions may also be used as models in crafting additional definitions.

Step Three: Goal Development

The next step in treatment plan development is to set broad goals for the resolution of the target problem. These statements need not be crafted in measurable terms but instead should focus on the long-term, global outcomes of treatment. Although *The Couples Psychotherapy Treatment Planner* suggests several possible goal statements for each problem, it is only necessary to select one goal for each treatment plan.

Step Four: Objective Construction

In contrast to long-term goals, objectives must be stated in behaviorally measurable language. It must be clear when the clients have achieved the established objectives. Review agencies (e.g., JCAHO), HMOs, and managed-care organizations insist that treatment results be measurable. The objectives presented in *The Couples Psychotherapy Treatment Planner* are designed to meet this demand for accountability. Numerous alternatives are presented to allow construction of a variety of treatment plan possibilities for the same presenting problem. The therapist must exercise professional judgment as to which objectives are most appropriate for a given couple.

Each objective should be developed as a step toward attaining the broad treatment goal. In essence, objectives can be thought of as a series of steps that, when completed, will result in the achievement of the long-term goal. There should be at least two objectives for each problem, but the therapist may select as many as are necessary for goal achievement. Target attainment dates should be listed for each objective. New objectives may be added to the plan as treatment progresses. Achieving all of the necessary objectives should signify resolution of the client's target problem and attainment of the written goal.

Step Five: Intervention Creation

Interventions are actions by the therapist designed to help the clients achieve the objectives. There should be at least one intervention for every objective. If the clients do not accomplish the objective after the initial intervention, new interventions should be added to the plan.

Interventions should be selected on the basis of the clients' needs and the therapist's full treatment repertoire. This *Couples Therapy Treatment Planner* contains interventions from a broad range of therapeutic approaches, including cognitive, dynamic, behavioral, pharmacological, family-oriented, experiential/expressive, and solution-focused brief therapy.

Step Six: Diagnosis Determination

The determination of an appropriate diagnosis is based on an evaluation of the clients' complete clinical presentation. The therapist must compare the behavioral, cognitive, emotional, and interpersonal symptoms presented by the clients to the criteria for diagnosis of a mental illness as described in DSM-IV. Careful assessment of behavioral indicators facilitates more accurate diagnosis and more effective treatment planning.

HOW TO USE THIS PLANNER

Learning the skills of effective treatment plan writing can be a tedious and difficult process for many therapists. *The Couples Psychotherapy Treatment Planner* was developed as a tool to aid therapists in quickly writing treatment plans that are clear, specific, and customized to the particular needs of each couple. Treatment plans should be developed by moving in turn through each of the following steps:

1. Choose one presenting problem (Step One) from those identified in the assessment process. Locate the corresponding page number for that problem in *The Couples Psychotherapy Treatment Planner*'s table of contents.
2. Select two or three of the listed behavioral definitions (Step Two) and record them in the appropriate section on the treatment plan form.
3. Select a single long-term goal (Step Three) and record it in the Goals section of the treatment plan form.
4. Review the listed objectives for this problem and select the ones clinically indicated for the clients (Step Four). Remember, it is recommended that at least two objectives be selected for each problem. Add a target date or the number of sessions allocated for the attainment of each objective.
5. Choose relevant interventions (Step Five). *The numbers of the interventions most salient to each objective are listed in parentheses following the objective statement.* Feel free to choose other interventions from the list, or to add new interventions as needed in the space provided.

6. DSM-IV diagnoses that are commonly associated with the problem are listed at the end of each chapter. These diagnoses are suggestions for clinical consideration. Select a diagnosis listed or assign a more appropriate choice from the DSM-IV (Step Six).

Note: To accommodate those practitioners who tend to plan treatment in terms of diagnostic labels rather than presenting problems, the Appendix lists all of the DSM-IV diagnoses that are included in the *Planner,* cross-referenced to the problems related to each diagnosis.

Following these steps will facilitate the development of complete, customized treatment plans, ready for immediate implementation and presentation to the clients. The final plan should resemble the format of the sample plan presented on the following two pages.

ELECTRONIC TREATMENT PLANNING

As paperwork mounts, more and more therapists are turning to computerized record keeping. The presenting problems, goals, objectives, interventions, and diagnoses in *The Couples Psychotherapy Treatment Planner* are available in electronic form as an add-on upgrade module to the popular software *TheraScribe® 3.0 for Windows®: The Computerized Assistant to Treatment Planning.* For more information on *Thera-Scribe* or *The Couples Psychotherapy* add-on module, call John Wiley & Sons at 1-800-879-4539, or mail the information request coupon at the back of this book.

A WORD OF CAUTION

Whether using the print *Planner* or the electronic version (*Thera-Scribe*), it is critical to remember that effective treatment planning requires that each plan be tailored to the specific problems and client's needs. *Treatment plans should not be mass-produced, even if clients have similar problems.* Each partner's and couple's strengths and weaknesses, unique stressors, social network, family circumstances, and interactional patterns *must* be considered in developing a treatment strategy. The clinically-derived statements in this *Planner* can be combined in thousands of permutations to develop detailed treatment plans. In addition, readers are encouraged add their own definitions, goals, objectives, and interventions to the existing samples.

SAMPLE TREATMENT PLAN

Problem: ANGER

Definitions: Uncontrolled expressions of anger that are perceived by the other partner as hurtful or threatening to the partner.

One partner continues to feel threatened even when the other believes that expressions of anger have modulated.

Yelling, cursing, and throwing or breaking of objects.

Goals: Learn to recognize the gradations of anger and when to intervene with other partner for maximum effectiveness.

Organize thoughts and behavior to increase the probability of desired outcomes without aggressive expressions of anger.

Learn to recognize and verbally express hurt feelings instead of expressing them through angry outbursts.

Objectives

1. Verbally identify the ways in which he/she is reinforced either immediately or later for getting angry. (6/22/98)

2. Identify successful and unsuccessful anger-management strategies of the past and their consequences. (7/7/98)

3. Identify anger episodes where the goal was to get something. (7/14/98)

Interventions

1. Have each partner describe how his/her anger gains something in the long term.

1. Ask how each partner has tried to manage or de-escalate his/her anger in ways that have been counterproductive.

2. Ask how each partner has tried to manage or de-escalate his/her anger in ways that have worked well in the past.

1. Have partners verbally identify episodes in which their anger was intended to get something (i.e., anger that results in getting one's way or anger that results from frustration over not getting one's way).

(Continued)

4. Practice the use of time-out techniques to modulate anger. (7/21/98).

1. Teach partners the six components of time-out technique (i.e., *self-monitoring* for escalating feelings of anger and hurt, *signaling* to the partner that verbal engagement should end, *acknowledging* the need of the partner to disengage, *separating* to disengage, *cooling down* to regain control of anger, and *returning* to controlled verbal engagement).

Diagnosis: 309.3 Adjustment Disorder With Disturbance of Conduct
V61.10 Partner Relational Problem

ALCOHOL ABUSE

BEHAVIORAL DEFINITIONS

1. Frequent use of alcohol by one or both partners, in large enough qualities to meet a diagnosis of alcohol abuse or alcohol dependence (e.g., interference in major role obligations, recurrent use in spite of danger to self, or health, legal, vocational and/or social problems).
2. Many arguments between partners over the issue of the alcohol abuser's continuing pattern of drinking.
3. Consistent failure of partner with alcohol abuse to keep repeated promises to quit or significantly reduce frequency and quantity of drinking.
4. Periodic episodes of violence or threats of physical harm, especially when the partner with alcohol abuse is intoxicated.
5. Significant deterioration of the relationship due to the effects of alcohol abuse (e.g., there is little or no communication, shared recreation, mutually satisfying sexual intercourse, or attempts to meet each other's emotional needs).
6. The partner without alcohol abuse consistently enables the partner with alcohol abuse by making excuses for the other's drinking, doing anything to please him/her, and denying the seriousness of the problem, while allowing self to be disparaged or abused repeatedly without offering assertive, constructive resistance.
7. Financial pressures (e.g., indebtedness, behind on rent, no savings) due to alcohol abuse, squandering of money, loss of jobs, and/or low-wage employment.

Special Caution: Conjoint treatment generally is not advisable for individuals with alcohol dependence that requires detoxification. In such cases, inpatient alcoholism rehabilitation or a detoxification program is first in order (see O'Farrell, 1993).

8. Social isolation. (e.g., the partner with alcohol abuse drinks too frequently and/or visits only with fellow alcohol users, and the other partner becomes passively withdrawn).

___. _____

   _____

   _____

___. _____

   _____

   _____

___. _____

   _____

LONG-TERM GOALS

1. Partner with alcohol abuse accepts the need for abstinence and actively participates in a recovery program.
2. Partner with alcohol abuse consistently and significantly reduces frequency and amount of alcohol consumption, such that no negative effects remain.
3. Quality of the relationship improves through a focus on support for sobriety, improved communication, and more frequent enjoyable social and sexual interactions.
4. Partner without alcohol abuse supports other partner's recovery and become more assertive, independent, and free from denial.
5. Partners establish a relationship of mutual trust and respect that is free of violence and has a pattern of seeking to meet each other's needs.
6. Partners address the impact that alcohol use has had on the relationship and engage in problem-solving to address ways the relationship will need to change when alcohol use is reduced or eliminated.
7. Partner without alcohol abuse reduces argumentativeness about the need to stop drinking, and partner with alcohol abuse learns to address the problem.

___. _____

   _____

   _____

___. _____

   _____

   _____

___. _____

   _____

SHORT-TERM OBJECTIVES

1. Describe the negative effects of alcohol abuse on self-esteem, family, work, social relationships, health, recreation, and finances. (1)

2. Partner with alcohol abuse signs a controlled-drinking contract as a means of assessing his/her ability to limit alcohol consumption to moderate levels. (2)

3. Partner with alcohol abuse reads material on controlled drinking. (3)

4. Both partners attend sessions alcohol-free. (4)

5. Both partners sign a nonviolence contract, and a safety plan is developed for the partner without alcohol abuse. (5, 6)

6. Partners agree to attend conjoint individual sessions. (7)

7. Identify the perceived or sought-after benefits of alcohol intoxication. (8)

8. Identify nondrinking behavioral alternatives that can produce the results sought after in alcohol abuse. (9)

9. Partner with alcohol abuse practices anxiety- or stress-reduction techniques that can be substituted for alcohol abuse. (10)

10. Partner with alcohol abuse practices anger-management strategies

THERAPEUTIC INTERVENTIONS

1. Have both partners describe the negative effects of alcohol abuse on the relationship and family, in individual sessions *before* conjoint treatment begins (to avoid the effects of intimidation and mutual supported denial).

2. Have the partner with alcohol abuse sign a controlled-drinking contract that stipulates the frequency of drinking allowed per week (e.g., twice) and the maximum number of drinks per instance (e.g., three in two hours). If this contract is broken three times, a nondrinking contract will be signed.

3. Assign partner with alcohol abuse to read information on controlled drinking. Examples include NIAAA pamphlet *How to Cut Down on Your Drinking* and/or *How to Control Your Drinking* (Miller & Munoz, 1982).

4. Require that both partners attend sessions alcohol-free. Enforce rule firmly and consistently by terminating session if it becomes apparent that alcohol has been recently consumed and is still in the bloodstream.

5. Have both partners sign a nonviolence contract that prohibits the use of physi-

that can be substituted for alcohol abuse and violence. (11, 12)

11. Understand and identify the social and biological causes for alcoholism that apply to situation. (13)

12. Partner with alcohol abuse signs a nondrinking contract. (14)

13. Partner with alcohol abuse agrees to a more intense level of treatment. (15, 16)

14. List actions the other partner could perform that would please self. Other partner agrees to do these things as a means of giving of self. (17)

15. Agree on a list of recreational activities to be enjoyed together and how they will be planned and implemented. (18)

16. Each partner lists ways that he/she interferes with healthy, open, communication between partners. (19, 20)

17. Demonstrate listening and empathy skills in a communication exercise. (21)

18. Each partner identifies at least one instance since the last session when he/she was listened to and understood by the other partner. (22)

19. Describe a problem in the relationship in a nonblaming, nonhostile manner. (23)

cally assaultive contact or weapons, or threats of same.

6. If individual treatment is in order to address anger issues before conjoint treatment, provide supportive counseling to the partner without alcohol abuse to address his/her anxiety and self-blame. Devise a safety plan to deal with partner's violence.

7. Discuss the appropriateness of couple and/or individual treatment. If violence is severe and has caused injury and/or significant fear, recommend individual treatment for the physically abusive partner before conjoint treatment is implemented.

8. Probe the benefits (e.g., reduced social anxiety, altered mood, lessened family demands) the partner with alcohol abuse is seeking in becoming intoxicated.

9. Assist in identifying constructive behavioral alternatives to produce the results sought in becoming intoxicated.

10. Teach partner with alcohol abuse the use of anxiety- or stress-reduction techniques (e.g., deep muscle relaxation, aerobic exercise, verbalization of concerns, positive guided imagery, recreational diversions, hot bath).

20. Practice problem-solving techniques within the session. (24)

21. Identify at least one instance since the last session when partners made cooperative use of problem-solving techniques learned in session. (25)

22. Partner with alcohol abuse apologizes (makes amends) to each family member for the distress he/she has caused. (26)

23. Identify triggers to episodes of drinking, and agree to alternative, nondrinking responses to cope with situations. (27, 28)

24. The nondrinking partner acknowledges his/her role as an enabler of the continuation of the alcohol abuse. (29)

25. The partner without alcohol abuse identifies instances when he/she has asserted self and refused to take responsibility for the behavior or feelings of the partner with alcohol abuse. (30, 31)

26. The partner without alcohol abuse confronts the other partner's irresponsible, abusive, or disrespectful behavior. (30, 31)

27. Partners discuss income and financial obligations and then formulate a budget to meet expenses. (32)

28. Partners identify opportunities that exist for social

11. Teach partner with alcohol abuse anger-management techniques (e.g., time out, thought-stopping, positive thought substitution, countdown serial 7s from 100).

12. Teach partners assertiveness as a healthy alternative to aggression.

13. Educate partners regarding the social and biological factors that contribute to alcoholism. Assign reading, including *Alcoholism: Getting the Facts* (NIAAA, 1996) and *I'll Quit Tomorrow* (Johnson, 1980).

14. Have partner with alcohol abuse sign a nondrinking contract that stipulates complete abstinence, cooperation with counseling, and attendance at AA meetings at least twice per week (daily, if necessary).

15. Require that if partner with alcohol abuse violates nondrinking contract, conjoint treatment will end unless he/she describes explicit steps (e.g., daily AA meetings, detox treatment, inpatient or IOP treatment) that he/she will take in the next week to become abstinent.

16. If drinking continues despite psychological intervention, provide physician referrals for Antabuse treatment and/or referrals for more intense alcoholism treatment (e.g., residential, inpatient, or IOP treatment).

interaction with other couples and develop a plan together for initiating contact for activities that do not involve alcohol consumption. (33)

—. _____
   _____
—. _____
   _____
—. _____
   _____

17. Assign each partner to do favors (even small ones) that will be appreciated by the other partner (e.g., help with or do a chore, run an errand, purchase a small present).

18. Encourage partners to engage in shared recreational activities (e.g., a family outing, visiting friends together), stipulating who is responsible for what steps in implementing the activity.

19. Have each partner describe the ways that he/she interferes with the communication process in the relationship (e.g., raises voice, walks away, refuses to respond, changes subject, calls partner names, uses profanity, becomes threatening).

20. Assist partners in self-exploration about their own communication styles and how they may have learned such styles from their family-of-origin experiences.

21. Choose a relationship conflict topic (e.g., child discipline, finances, assigning home chores) and have couple discuss it in session. Assess and provide feedback on partners' listening and communication styles to improve healthy, accurate, effective communication.

22. Review and reinforce positive communication experiences between the partners

that occurred since the last session.

23. Encourage partners to describe a problem between them in a nonblaming, nonhostile manner. Give feedback and guidance using modeling and role-playing.

24. Model and role-play problem-solving discussions using the following steps: (*a*) define the problem (with the help of the therapist); (*b*) generate many solutions, even if some are not practical, encouraging creativity; (*c*) evaluate the proposed solutions; (*d*) implement the solutions.

25. Review and reinforce partners' reported instances of implementing problem-solving techniques at home since the last session.

26. Encourage partner with alcohol abuse to make amends by apologizing to each family member for specific behaviors that have caused distress.

27. Assist partners in identifying situations that trigger relapses of drinking episodes.

28. Assist partner with alcohol abuse in developing positive alternative coping behaviors (e.g., calling a sponsor, attending an AA meeting, practicing stress-reduction skills, turning problem over to a higher power) as reactions to trigger situations.

29. Confront the partner without alcohol abuse regarding behaviors that support the continuation of abusive drinking by other partner (e.g., lying to cover up for the drinker's irresponsibility, minimizing the seriousness of the drinking problem, taking on most of the family responsibilities, tolerating the verbal, emotional, and/or physical abuse).

30. Model and role-play examples of partner without alcohol abuse refusing to accept responsibility for the behavior and/or feelings of the other partner. Reinforce the partner without alcohol abuse for practicing this assertiveness in situations at home.

31. Encourage and reinforce instances of the partner without alcohol abuse confronting the partner with alcohol abuse for treating him/her with disrespect or blatant abuse.

32. Assign partners to discuss finances and prepare a mutually agreed upon budget that begins to deal with the financial stress caused by drinking problem.

33. Encourage and assist partners in planning for non-alcohol-consuming social activities with other couples. Suggest church, hobby, and recreational groups or

work associates as possible
opportunities for social out-
reach.

___. _____

_____

___. _____

_____

___. _____

_____

DIAGNOSTIC SUGGESTIONS

Axis I: 303.90   Alcohol Dependence
                305.00   Alcohol Abuse
                300.4   Dysthymic Disorder
                V61.1   Partner Relational Problem

_____   _____

_____   _____

Axis II: 301.6   Dependent Personality Disorder
                301.82   Avoidant Personality Disorder

_____   _____

_____   _____

ANGER

BEHAVIORAL DEFINITIONS

1. Uncontrolled expressions of anger that are perceived by the other partner as hurtful or threatening.
2. One partner continues to feel threatened even when the other believes that expressions of anger have modulated.
3. Violating the rights of the other partner through attempts to enforce legitimate wishes via coercive means.
4. Yelling, cursing, and throwing or breaking of objects.

___. _____
_____

___. _____
_____

___. _____
_____

LONG-TERM GOALS

1. Learn to recognize the positive functions and negative consequences of current style of expressing and managing anger.

Extreme, out-of-control expressions of anger in a conjoint session can be especially detrimental to therapeutic progress. The therapist should assess the level of anger in individual sessions prior to any conjoint sessions. If outbursts in conjoint sessions become disruptive, individual sessions should be resumed until progress in anger control becomes evident. In most cases, the therapist should alert couples to the possibility of mixing individual and conjoint sessions as clinically indicated. Such alerts should be given *before* any problems occur, so that moving back to individual sessions does not appear to be punitive.

2. Learn to recognize the gradations of anger and when to intervene with other partner for maximum effectiveness.
3. Understand the different functions of anger, and learn to satisfy function-related needs in a more constructive manner.
4. Organize thoughts and behavior to increase desired outcomes without aggressive expressions of anger.
5. Support and care for each other when feeling hurt or vulnerable.
6. Learn to recognize and verbally express hurt feelings instead of expressing them through angry outbursts.

—. _____
   _____
—. _____
   _____
—. _____
   _____

SHORT-TERM OBJECTIVES

1. Verbalize an understanding of anger as an adaptive physiological response to fight a perceived threat. (1, 2, 3)
2. Verbally identify the short- and long-term destructive effects of current style of expressing anger. (4, 5)
3. Verbally identify the ways in which he/she is reinforced either immediately or later for getting angry. (6, 7)
4. Identify successful and unsuccessful anger-management strategies of the past and their conse- quences. (8, 9)
5. Identify ways in which one partner's anger-

THERAPEUTIC INTERVENTIONS

1. Educate partners that the purpose of anger control is not to eliminate anger, because anger is an impor- tant, natural signal that something important is at stake.
2. Educate partners that anger motivates the body's general response to fight a perceived threat and that the form these responses take can either help or hurt one's self and the relation- ship.
3. Educate partners that the goals of anger control are first to recognize the impor- tance of a provocative situa- tion, and then to manage anger in a way that

management strategies have been misinterpreted by the other. (10)

6. Both partners contract to manage their anger and use therapy constructively. (11, 12)

7. Contract to discuss angry feelings respectfully by balancing concern for the other partner's feelings with the need to express self. (13, 14)

8. Verbalize recognition of the gradations of anger cues in the three channels of anger (i.e., physiological, cognitive, and behavioral). (15, 16, 17, 18)

9. Identify the degree of anger (on a scale of 0–100) that in the past has led to destructive expressions of anger and lack of control. (19, 20, 21)

10. Practice the use of time-out techniques to modulate anger. (21, 22, 23)

11. Define the three main reasons for anger. (24)

12. Identify anger episodes where the goal was to get something. (25)

13. Identify anger episodes where the goal was to assert independence. (26)

14. Identify anger episodes where the goal was protection, or a reaction to a perceived injury. (27)

15. Track anger-eliciting situations at home and identify

strengthens rather than weakens the relationship.

4. Have each partner describe the ways in which his/her anger is destructive to self or relationship in the short term.

5. Have each partner describe the ways in which his/her anger is destructive to self or relationship in the long term.

6. Have each partner describe how his/her anger gains something in the short term.

7. Have each partner describe how his/her anger gains something in the long term.

8. Ask how each partner has tried to manage or de-escalate his/her anger in ways that have worked well in the past.

9. Ask how each partner has tried to manage or de-escalate his/her anger in ways that have been counterproductive.

10. Help partners identify ways in which one's de-escalation strategies have been perceived as a provocation to the other (e.g., male partner's withdrawal is perceived as provocative rejection by the female partner).

11. Have both partners contract to accept responsibility for managing own anger instead of managing the other's behavior.

the goal of the anger (to get something, to assert independence, or to protect self). (28, 29)

16. Organize a list of thoughts, behaviors, actual outcomes, and desired outcomes via situational analysis of anger experiences. (30, 31)

17. Verbalize interpretive thoughts that were unhelpful, global, or inaccurate, and then state more beneficial self-talk. (32, 33)

18. Report seeking outcomes over which he/she has control (versus those outcomes over which he/she has no control) in anger-eliciting situations. (34)

19. Identify self-corrective skills by stating lessons learned from situational analysis exercises. (35)

20. Contract to verbalize angry feelings instead of acting them out. (36)

21. Verbalize the differences between unassertive, assertive, and aggressive responses. (37)

22. Practice assertive behaviors until successful. (38, 39)

23. Verbally agree that neither partner will capitulate to the other's angry demands. (40)

24. Practice paraphrasing the other partner's appropriate expressions of upset. (41, 43)

25. Firmly but nonaggressively assert independence from

12. Have both partners contract to use therapy sessions for constructive purposes and to abide by the therapist's directions if the process becomes destructive.

13. Teach both partners the speaker skill of "measured truthfulness" (i.e., each balances the need to comment about the other against a concern for the other's feelings), and have them practice this skill on areas of conflict.

14. Increase emotional safety of sessions by having both partners contract to use "measured truthfulness" at home and in session when discussing anger-eliciting topics.

15. Assist partners in identifying the behavioral, cognitive, and affective cues of being at low levels of anger (0–30 on a 0–100 scale).

16. Assist partners in identifying the behavioral, cognitive, and affective cues that their anger is increasing into the moderate level of anger (31–50 on a 0–100 scale).

17. Assist partners in identifying the behavioral, cognitive, and affective cues that their anger is increasing into the danger zone of anger (51–70 on a 0–100 scale).

18. Assist partners in identifying the behavioral, cognitive, and affective cues that

the other partner's coercive control. (42)

26. Recognize and verbalize "softer" emotions (sadness, disappointment, hurt, fear, vulnerability) that precede anger. (44)

27. Deal with a perceived need for protection by verbalizing the need and requesting care instead of becoming defensively aggressive. (45, 46, 47)

28. Reflect and empathize with the other partner's vulnerabilities and hurts. (48, 49)

—. _____
_____

—. _____
_____

—. _____
_____

their anger is increasing into the extreme zone of anger, where emotional and/or physical abusiveness becomes more likely (71–100 on a 0–100 scale).

19. Inquire at what levels anger has been constructive and destructive in the past.

20. Inquire at what level of anger effective control over behavior begins to erode.

21. Identify at what level of anger the management skills should be exercised.

22. Teach partners the six components of time-out technique (i.e., *self-monitoring* for escalating feelings of anger and hurt, *signaling* to the partner that verbal engagement should end, *acknowledging* the need of the partner to disengage, *separating* to disengage, *cooling down* to regain control of anger, and *returning* to controlled verbal engagement).

23. Coach couple during practice attempts of time out, and assign at-home practice.

24. Teach partners the three main reasons for anger: (*a*) to get something, (*b*) to assert independence, and (*c*) to protect self (Notarius and Markman, 1993).

25. Have partners verbally identify episodes in which their anger was intended to get something (i.e., anger that results in getting one's

way, or anger that results from frustration over not getting one's way).

26. Have partners verbally identify episodes in which their anger was intended to assert independence (i.e., anger that results from perceptions that the other partner is trying to exert control over one's life or actions).

27. Have partners verbally identify episodes in which their anger was intended for protection (i.e., anger that results from perceptions that one is hurt or vulnerable).

28. Assign anger-tracking homework that (a) lists the situations that trigger anger, (b) identifies which of the three goals that applies, and (c) recounts the thoughts and behaviors that occur during such anger-eliciting situations.

29. Have partners review their anger-tracking homework and identify those situations where they were trying to get something, those where they were asserting independence, and those where they felt the need to protect themselves.

30. Using individual sessions as needed, have a partner choose from his/her homework specific anger-eliciting situations and tell what his/her interpretations/cognitions were, what his/her

behavior was, and what the
actual outcome of the situation was (i.e., demonstrate
how to organize a situa-
tional analysis).

31. As the concluding step in the
situational analysis, have
the partner describe what
his/her desired outcome was
in the specified situation.

32. Help partner determine
whether each thought was
(a) helpful in getting the
desired outcome, (b)
anchored to the specific
situation described (i.e., is
situationally-specific instead
of global), and (c) accurate
(i.e., overt evidence could be
marshaled to support it).

33. If any thoughts are not productive, anchored, and accurate, have partner reword
the thoughts so they meet
criteria. (For example,
"She's always on my back
about spending time with
the kids," can become "She's
exhausted and is looking for
a break.")

34. Help partner determine
whether the desired out-
come was achievable (i.e.,
under his/her control). If
not, have partner reword
the desired outcome so that
it becomes achievable. (For
example, "I want him to listen to me when I'm upset,"
can become "I want to ask
him to schedule a time for
us to talk about problems
that we're having.")

35. Have partner summarize the situation by deriving a lesson to be learned from the situational analysis.

36. Ask partners to agree to label and talk about angry feelings instead of acting them out.

37. Distinguish differences between being unassertive (i.e., not standing up for one's wishes or rights), assertive (i.e., appropriately asserting one's wishes or rights without infringing on the rights of others), and aggressive (i.e., asserting one's wishes or rights without regard to the rights of others).

38. For "get-something" desired outcomes, have speaker practice assertive (not aggressive) communication skills such as "I" statements. (See Communication chapter of this *Planner.*)

39. Reinforce assertiveness behaviors in session and reports of successful assertiveness between sessions.

40. For "get-something" desired outcomes, have both partners verbally agree that neither partner is obligated to give in to the angry wishes of the other.

41. For "get-something" desired outcomes, have the listener paraphrase the speaker's message, focusing on the speaker's implicit or explicit

desired outcome and not the angry affect.

42. For "assert independence" desired outcomes, have the speaker practice assertive (not aggressive) communication skills that identify the specific behaviors that trigger their perceptions of being controlled.

43. For "assert independence" desired outcomes, have the listener paraphrase the speaker's message, focusing on the speaker's perceptions and not the listener's desire to defend his/her actions.

44. For "protection" desired outcomes, have the speaker identify emotions that precede anger (e.g., hurt, fearful, or vulnerable).

45. For "protection" desired outcomes, have the speaker practice making "I" statements that acknowledge his/her personal vulnerabilities.

46. For "protection" desired outcomes, have the speaker practice taking responsibility for protecting him/herself in a manner that does not attack the other partner.

47. For "protection" desired outcomes, have the speaker practice making requests for support and caring from the other partner when hurt, fearful, or vulnerable.

48. For "protection" desired outcomes, have the listener

reflect the underlying emotion felt by the speaker
when hurt or vulnerable.

49. If listener responds defensively, have partners switch
places and ask listener to
verbalize the other partner's
perspective and feelings.

___. _____

_____

___. _____

_____

___. _____

_____

DIAGNOSIS SUGGESTIONS

Axis I	309.0	Adjustment Disorder With Depressed Mood
	309.3	Adjustment Disorders With Disturbance of Conduct
	305.00	Alcohol Abuse
	303.90	Alcohol Dependence
	296.x	Bipolar I Disorder
	296.x	Major Depressive Disorder
	V61.1	Partner Relational Problem
	V61.1	Physical Abuse of Adult, 995.81 Victim
	V61.21	Physical Abuse of Child, 995.5 Victim
	_____	_____
	_____	_____
Axis II	301.7	Antisocial Personality Disorder
	301.83	Borderline Personality Disorder
	301.81	Narcissistic Personality Disorder
	_____	_____
	_____	_____

ANXIETY

BEHAVIORAL DEFINITIONS

1. Repeated experiences of perceived threat and worry that impede normal fulfillment of important roles.
2. One or both partners experience disruptions severe enough to meet a diagnosis of an anxiety disorder (excessive and unwarranted worry, motor tension, autonomic hyperactivity, hypervigilance).
3. Arguments over the anxiety problem, or over the adaptations that it has forced both partners to make.
4. Social isolation, caused by the anxiety problem, that is distressing to one or both partners.
5. Lengthy, repetitive discussions of worry that do not reduce the anxiety, or are irritating to the other partner.

__. _____
   _____
__. _____
   _____
__. _____
   _____

LONG-TERM GOALS

1. Learn to recognize anxiety problems and to overcome them using cognitive and behavioral coping strategies.
2. Support each other in overcoming the anxiety problem.
3. Participate together in exposure and response-prevention sessions to reduce the anxious partner's distress.

4. Replace anxiety-producing cognitions with healthy, realistic self-talk.
5. Actively schedule and participate in anxiety- and stress-reducing activities, both individually and together.
6. Learn to communicate with each other about positive coping, and to limit discussions about worries.

—. _____
   _____
—. _____
   _____
—. _____
   _____

SHORT-TERM OBJECTIVES

1. Verbally identify the triggers for and symptoms of the current anxiety problem. (1, 3)
2. Verbally track the ways in which the anxiety problem has changed across time. (2)
3. List the ways that the anxiety problem has impacted on each partner individually. (4, 6)
4. List the ways that the anxiety problem has impacted on the couple's relationship. (5, 7)
5. Articulate current attempts at coping with the anxiety problem. (8)
6. Describe how support for the partner with anxiety problem by the partner without anxiety problem has changed across time. (9)

THERAPEUTIC INTERVENTIONS

1. Have partner with anxiety problem describe the anxiety and avoidance symptoms that he/she is experiencing.
2. Have partner with anxiety problem describe the developmental course of the anxiety problem.
3. Ask partner without anxiety problem to provide his/her perspective on the other partner's anxiety and avoidance symptoms. (This input may bring to light other anxiety or avoidance symptoms that have not previously been mentioned.)
4. Have partner with anxiety problem describe the effect that his/her problem has had on self.
5. Ask partner with anxiety problem to describe the

7. Describe the ways in which the anxiety problem produces a relationship conflict. (10)

8. Describe how the anxiety problem has changed the ways in which required roles are fulfilled. (11, 12)

9. Verbalize an understanding of anxiety as an adaptive physiological response to fight or flee from a perceived threat, but one that has advantages and disadvantages. (13, 14)

10. Verbalize an understanding of the principal that anxiety can be broken by testing the accuracy of feelings of threat. (15, 16)

11. Practice exposing self to the avoided stimulus situation in gradual steps of time and intensity, while monitoring actual versus imagined feelings of threat. (17)

12. Verbalize recognition of the three channels of anxiety—physiological, cognitive, and behavioral. (18)

13. Read instructional material about panic disorder. (19)

14. Read instructional material about generalized anxiety disorder. (20)

15. Contract for partner without anxiety problem to serve as coach for the other partner, assisting in anticipation of anxiety-producing situations and prompting the use of coping strategies. (21, 22)

effect that his/her problem has had on the couple's relationship.

6. Ask partner without anxiety problem to describe the effect the other partner's problem has had on him/her individually.

7. Ask partner without anxiety problem to describe the effect the other partner's problem has had on the couple's relationship.

8. Have both partners describe how they currently are attempting to cope with the anxiety problem.

9. Ask partner without anxiety problem to describe how his/her supportiveness about the problem has changed across time.

10. Guide the couple in discussing the ways in which the anxiety problem may precipitate relationship conflicts.

11. Have both partners describe how the anxiety problem has affected their current role arrangement.

12. Guide the couple in discussing how the current role arrangement came about. Did they discuss their current responsibility allocations overtly, or did the current arrangement evolve implicitly?

13. Educate partners that anxiety motivates the body's general response to fight or flee perceived threats, and

16. Recognize and rate the gradations of the anxiety experienced. (23, 24, 25)

17. Contract to use severity of anxiety ratings as a shorthand, low-key way to communicate with other partner about anxiety in public. (26)

18. Verbalize the difference, at increasing levels of anxiety, in anxiety cues in the physiological, cognitive, and behavioral channels. (27, 28, 29, 30)

19. Practice using diaphragmatic, deep breathing to reduce anxiety. (31, 32)

20. Identify and rank in order feared situations that occur in the natural environment. (33, 34)

21. Practice exposing self to feared situations in session and at home while avoiding the use of maladaptive coping responses (e.g., withdrawal). (35, 36)

22. Practice challenging anxiety-eliciting cognitions that overestimate threat. (37, 38, 39)

23. Practice challenging anxiety-eliciting cognitions that catastrophize. (40, 41, 42)

24. Schedule anxiety-reducing activities that can be done individually. (43)

25. Schedule anxiety reducing activities that can be done with partner. (44)

26. Engage in positive discussions about the future. (45)

that the form these responses take can either help or hurt the self and relationship.

14. Educate partners that while anxiety can serve a useful protective function, overuse of this defense mechanism can exhaust both an individual and a relationship.

15. Educate partners that to break an anxiety habit, one must face feared situations to test whether the feared consequences are real or overestimated. Due to generalization, appropriate anxiety resulting from a specific, high-threat situation in the past often gets reapplied to new, low-threat situations.

16. Explain to couple that to truly break an anxiety habit, successful exposure to feared situations must prevent the client with anxiety problem from using maladaptive coping responses (e.g., escape). Exposure also must be long enough and regular enough for the anxiety to subside (i.e., the behavioral principle of habituation).

17. Encourage client with anxiety problem to face a specific anxiety-producing situation in gradually increasing steps of time and intensity without using escape. During exposure, have partner with anxiety

27. Report on the success of limiting discussions about anxiety to set times of limited duration. (46)

—. _____
   _____
—. _____
   _____
—. _____
   _____

problem monitor actual versus imagined feelings of threat while other partner gently encourages him/her.

18. Educate partners that anxiety operates through three channels—behavioral, cognitive, and affective/physiological.

19. Assign both partners to read *Mastering Your Anxiety and Panic—Patient's Workbook* (Barlow and Craske, 1994).

20. Assign both partners to read *Mastering Your Anxiety and Worry—Patient's Workbook* (Craske and Barlow, et al.)

21. Determine whether partner with anxiety problem would feel comfortable with other partner serving as coach. (If both clients are anxious, ask if each can serve as coach for the other.)

22. With the partner without anxiety problem serving as coach, have the couple anticipate potential problems and brainstorm ways to avoid them. Have both partners contract to use the relationship as a source of help and strength in conquering the problem.

23. Educate partners that anxiety is not an on/off phenomenon, but rather one of gradations.

24. Teach couple to use the Subjective Units of Discom-

fort (SUDS) scale, in which
partner with anxiety problem rates perceived anxiety
on a 0–100 scale.

25. Have partner with anxiety
problem describe for the
other partner what his/her
current SUDS score is, what
elements of the situation
are affecting the SUDS, and
what internal cues he/she is
using to determine the
SUDS.

26. Have partners contract to
discreetly use SUDS scores
to signal to each other the
level of anxiety being experienced in various situations.

27. Ask partner with anxiety
problem to verbalize to
other partner the behav-
ioral, cognitive, and affective cues of experiencing
low levels of anxiety (0–30
on a 0–100 scale).

28. Ask partner with anxiety
problem to verbalize to
other partner the behav-
ioral, cognitive, and affective cues that signal anxiety
is increasing into the moderate level (31–50 on a
0–100 scale).

29. Ask partner with anxiety
problem to verbalize to
other partner the behav-
ioral, cognitive, and affective cues that signal anxiety
is increasing into the high
moderate zone (51–70 on a
0–100 scale).

30. Ask partner with anxiety
problem to verbalize to

other partner the behavioral, cognitive, and affective cues that signal anxiety is increasing into the extreme zone (71–100 on a 0–100 scale).

31. Teach both partners diaphragmatic breathing, including the skills of (a) differentiating diaphragmatic breathing from chest breathing, (b) taking deep breaths, (c) inhaling slowly and deeply for 5 seconds while thinking the word "calm," and (d) exhaling for 10 seconds. Partner without anxiety problem should learn diaphragmatic breathing both to learn tension management for own benefit and to be a supportive coach to the other partner.

32. Assign both partners to individually practice diaphragmatic breathing for three 10-minute sessions each day. Assign them to record the time and date, their SUDS score prior to the practice session, and their score following the session.

33. Assign anxiety-tracking homework that uses a written journal to identify the situations that trigger anxiety as well as the thoughts and behaviors that occur during anxiety-eliciting situations.

34. Identify feared situations, have partner with anxiety

problem generate estimated SUDS score for each situation, and generate a hierarchical list of feared situations.

35. Conduct in session imagined exposure of the partner with anxiety problem to a feared situation, beginning at the lower end of the hierarchy. Model for other partner how to ask for SUDS ratings every several minutes and how to be encouraging during the exposure.

36. Assign couple to conduct *in vivo* exposures at home, to record the SUDS scores, and to note any problems encountered.

37. Define *probability overestimation* (the belief that relatively rare, feared events happen more frequently than they actually do) for the couple.

38. Model dialogue that challenges probability overestimation. Have the partner with anxiety problem estimate the probability of a feared event happening (e.g., son getting hurt in a car accident). Focus on the evidence to support such estimations (e.g., "So, if the probability of Fred being in an accident were 50 percent, one out of every two trips would involve an accident. Does it happen that frequently?").

39. Have the partner without anxiety problem calmly discuss probability overestimation with the other partner in a manner similar to that previously modeled by the therapist.

40. Define *catastrophizing* (magnifying insignificant consequences out of proportion) for the couple.

41. Model self-talk or partner dialogue that challenges catastrophizing by the partner with anxiety problem. Ask him/her to imagine the worst-case scenario, and discuss how the couple would cope with such an event.

42. Ask partner without anxiety problem to discuss catastrophizing with the other partner in a calm manner similar to that modeled by the therapist.

43. Have both partners commit to and schedule regular individual stress-reducing activities, such as diaphragmatic breathing or deep-muscle relaxation techniques, exercise, music, or hobbies.

44. Ask each partner to identify actions that he/she could take to be a source of support and anxiety reduction to the other partner. Have them commit to and schedule regular couple anxiety- and stress-reducing activities, such as

foot rubs, back rubs, social engagements, walks, sex, or shared hobbies.

45. Have the couple engage in confident discussions about the future, both in session and at home, focusing on planning and coping for future events.

46. Assign couple to schedule set times for brief "worry meetings" to discuss anxieties. Airing of anxieties should be limited to these meetings.

—. _____
_____

—. _____
_____

—. _____
_____

DIAGNOSTIC SUGGESTIONS

Axis I	293.89	Anxiety Disorder Due to . . . [indicate the general medical condition]
	300.00	Anxiety Disorder NOS
	300.02	Generalized Anxiety Disorder
	300.21	Panic Disorder With Agoraphobia
	300.01	Panic Disorder Without Agoraphobia
	309.24	Adjustment Disorder With Anxiety
	309.28	Adjustment Disorder With Mixed Anxiety and Depressed Mood
	V61.1	Partner Relational Problem
	_____	_____
	_____	_____

BLAME

BEHAVIORAL DEFINITIONS

1. One partner repeatedly blames the other for the relationship problems and the relationship dissatisfaction (e.g., "If you weren't so crazy our marriage would be fine," or "Our whole problem is you and your ideas," or "If you would stop being so critical I'd be happy").
2. Both partners express dissatisfaction with the relationship.
3. The blaming partner is very resistant to examining his/her role in the conflict.
4. The blaming partner projects responsibility for his/her behavior, thoughts, and feelings onto the other partner.
5. Virtually all discussions result in being caught up in blaming rather than honest, open self-examination.
6. The blamed partner lacks consistent assertiveness and tends to terminate communication in a show of helplessness and frustration.
7. The blamed partner verbalizes feelings of low self-esteem and of not being valued by the other partner.

—. _____

_____

—. _____

_____

—. _____

_____

LONG-TERM GOALS

1. Eliminate or reduce the frequency of partner blame.
2. Reduce the anger that is often associated with blaming.
3. Reduce the frequency of critical comments often associated with blaming.
4. Help blaming partner develop a less-unidirectional view of the causes of relationship problems.

___. _____
_____
___. _____
_____
___. _____
_____

SHORT-TERM OBJECTIVES

1. Describe problems in the relationship in a respectful, calm manner. (1, 2, 3)

2. Each partner describe own actions that contribute to the identified problems (i.e., avoid projecting all blame on the other partner). (4, 5)

3. Verbalize problems in the present tense instead of focusing on issues of the past. (7, 8)

4. Verbalize concerns about the other partner's behavior by using "I" messages, rather than disparaging the other partner. (9)

5. Report an increase in respectful communication at home (i.e., discussions

THERAPEUTIC INTERVENTIONS

1. In individual sessions, have each partner describe the problems in the relationship. Discourage blaming and reinforce respectful descriptions of problems that have their basis in both partners' behavior.

2. Assess whether chemical dependence, physical or sexual abuse, or an extramarital affair is the basis for most of the blaming in the relationship. If so, employ guidelines from the appropriate *Treatment Planner* chapters to focus conflict resolution on that issue.

3. In conjoint sessions, use modeling and reframing to encourage each partner to

are open and free from hostility). (10)

6. Each partner identify two behaviors to engage in that will please the other partner. (6, 11, 12)

7. Report an increase in positive, complementary, appreciative comments made to other partner. (13)

8. Assume responsibility for own behavior, thoughts, and feelings. (14)

9. Blaming partner list positive behaviors desired by other partner (rather than pointing out negative behaviors that trigger criticism). (15)

10. Blamed partner agree to make efforts at engaging in positive behaviors that will please the other partner. (16)

11. Blaming partner list times blamed partner has been praised for pleasing changes in behavior. (17)

12. List the "basic rules" of the relationship that cause hurt, anger, and blaming when they are violated. (18, 19)

13. Agree to a renegotiated set of "basic rules" that will increase satisfaction with the relationship if adhered to. (20)

14. List external stressors that put pressure on the relationship and lead to blaming. (21)

15. Engage in problem-solving discussions with other part-

state problems in a respectful, noncondemning manner.

4. Encourage and reinforce each partner's taking responsibility for how he/she contributes to the problems rather than projecting all blame on the other partner.

5. Have each partner sign a therapeutic agreement indicating that he/she is partly responsible for the satisfaction and/or dissatisfaction in the relationship.

6. Have each of the partners separately present some problems, however minor, for which they feel they can admit partial responsibility and can agree to make constructive changes.

7. Using modeling and praise, encourage and reinforce both partners' efforts at focusing on current problems rather than fixating on the distant past.

8. Encourage the blaming partner to give up anger about a hurt from the distant past and to practice forgiveness that heals, rather than bitterness that divides.

9. Using role-playing and modeling, reinforce the use of "I" messages (i.e., stating first what thoughts and feelings were experienced, before stating the partner's behavior that seemed to trigger those thoughts and feelings).

ner and then verbalize agreement on how to constructively cope with external stressors (rather than reacting with anger and blaming). (22)

—. _____
_____
—. _____
_____
—. _____
_____

10. Using role-playing and modeling, encourage assertiveness versus passiveness or aggressiveness as an effective means of expressing thoughts and feelings.

11. Have each partner stipulate and then engage in two behaviors that he/she feels would be appreciated by the other partner, in order to provide some clear examples of how each can take responsibility for increasing satisfaction in the relationship.

12. Have each partner report on a positive interchange that reflects change and improvement in the relationship. Reinforce each instance of positive interaction, highlighting what contributes to its being pleasant.

13. Assign each partner to express appreciation for two things each day that are pleasing to him/her about the other partner's behavior.

14. Teach the partners that each is responsible for his/her own behavior, thoughts, and feelings, as each has a myriad of choices as a reaction to the other's behavior.

15. Assign the blaming partner to list positive behaviors that the blamed partner could engage in to please the blaming partner (i.e., focus on the position that is desired rather than the negative that is criticized).

16. Solicit from the blamed partner an agreement to make a reasonable, sincere effort to please the other partner.

17. Have the blaming partner review occasions when he/she has complimented behavior in the other partner. Encourage and reinforce the blaming partner for shifting to a position of praise from one of criticism.

18. Assist each partner in articulating the "basic rules" of the couple's relationship (for example, that the husband should help to put the children to bed, and the wife should assist in yard work).

19. Clarify how "rules of the relationship" are being broken and how those rule violations evoke negative feelings.

20. Assist both partners in renegotiating rules and roles that are agreeable to each, as a means of reducing blaming behavior.

21. Have each partner list the external stressors that are putting pressure on the couple's relationship.

22. Aid partners in using problem-solving techniques as a means of coping with external pressures as a team, rather than shifting all the responsibility to one partner.

—. _____
   _____
—. _____
   _____
—. _____
   _____

DIAGNOSTIC SUGGESTIONS

Axis I: 309.24   Adjustment Disorder With Anxiety
               309.0   Adjustment Disorder With Depressed Mood
               309.3   Adjustment Disorder With Disturbance of
                        Conduct
               309.28   Adjustment Disorder With Mixed Anxiety and
                        Depressed Mood
               309.4   Adjustment Disorder With Mixed Disturbance
                        of Emotions and Conduct
               305.00   Alcohol Abuse
               303.90   Alcohol Dependence
               296.xx   Major Depressive Disorder
               312.34   Intermittent Explosive Disorder
               V61.1   Partner Relational Problem
               _____   _____
               _____   _____

Axis II: 301.0   Paranoid Personality Disorder
               301.7   Antisocial Personality Disorder
               301.83   Borderline Personality Disorder
               301.81   Narcissistic Personality Disorder
               _____   _____
               _____   _____

BLENDED-FAMILY PROBLEMS

BEHAVIORAL DEFINITIONS

1. Frequent arguments between parent and stepparent over child-discipline differences.
2. Frequent arguments between partners over favoritism or financial and gift supports for biological versus nonbiological children.
3. Financial pressures and resentment about the financial aspects of divorce settlements.
4. Parental jealousy and sibling rivalry stemming from differences in the social and emotional development of the children from two different marriages.
5. Concerns about leaving opposite-sex teenage step-siblings alone together (i.e., concerns about sexual activity or sex abuse).
6. Suspicions by female partner that male partner is sexually attracted to her daughter.

Families in the twenty-first century often will be outside what has been called the traditional or nuclear family. There is no clear agreement on words used to describe families characterized by one adult with at least one child from a previous union who establishes a household with someone who has no legal ties with that child. In this *Treatment Planner,* we choose to use the words "blended family" and "combined family" to characterize such families. Combined families include individuals related by blood (parents and children) and individuals related by marriage (stepparents and stepchildren). According to demographer Paul Glick, by the year 2000 approximately 50 percent of children and adults will be in blended families (Kaufman, 1993, *The Combined Family*). Although combined families are becoming increasingly common, the odds are 6 in 10 that remarriages with children will end in divorce. Thus, planning for the issues that naturally occur in blended/combined families is certainly prudent. This *Treatment Planner* is designed to aid a therapist in helping members of combined families.

7. Partner-conflicts about visitation and transportation to and from noncustodial ex-partner's home (e.g., ex-partner's lateness in picking up a child, ex-partner's failure to show up for visitation, ex-partner who enters home to get a child).
8. Distrust and jealousy regarding other partner's suspected emotional and/or sexual connection to ex-partner.
9. Internalizing and/or externalizing child-behavior problems.

—. _____
_____
—. _____
_____
—. _____
_____

LONG-TERM GOALS

1. All members of the combined family treat each other with mutual respect, equality, and fairness.
2. Partners trust each other's loyalty, love, and commitment, and work cooperatively on child-rearing.
3. Communication with ex-partners regarding children occurs frequently and without major disagreements.
4. Partners resolve jealousy, hurt, and anger toward their ex-partners.
5. Each partner develops understanding about the dilemmas and conflicts that the other experiences with his/her ex-partner.
6. The nonbiological parent learns to establish a respectful, appropriate relationship with the other partner's child or children.
7. Partners accept the financial constraints (e.g., support and maintenance payments, expense sharing) imposed by their respective divorce settlements.
8. Disciplinary actions by a nonbiological parent occur only after a relationship has been established between that parent and the child.
9. Children resolve their loyalty conflicts with parents who have divorced.

—. _____
_____

—. _____
   _____
   _____
—. _____
   _____

SHORT-TERM OBJECTIVES

1. Describe conflicts with ex-partners. (1)
2. Describe the guilt about ex-partner and about the dilemmas their children face because of a separation or divorce. (2, 3)
3. Review any implicit or explicit divorce or separation financial agreements and discuss their implications. (4, 5, 6, 9)
4. Discuss separate and conjoint finances openly, and agree about budgeting for expenses not covered in agreements. (7, 8, 9)
5. Discuss how to provide support that is in line with a separation or divorce agreement without that support appearing to be highly discrepant toward children from one family or the other. (4, 8)
6. Make explicit any implicit financial, child care, or visitation and transportation agreements that have evolved with ex-partners. (9)

THERAPEUTIC INTERVENTIONS

1. Ask partners to describe their feelings about and conflicts with their ex-partner.
2. Have partners relate the ways in which they experience conflict about dealing with their ex-partner.
3. Encourage partners to openly discuss their guilty feelings about the "failure" of the former relationships, and how these feelings affect their present relationship with their ex-partners and children.
4. Discuss the respective divorce and separation agreements, and have partners discuss the short- and long-term implications of these agreements.
5. Guide partners in discussing how they will cope with problems that may result from respective legal and/or financial agreements (e.g., a husband having to pay a large percentage of his salary to his ex-wife, leaving relatively little money for the combined family).

7. Agree on the nature and timing of a response to an ex-partner for a broken divorce agreement. (10)

8. Verbalize feelings about and acceptance of visitation agreement that the biological parent has with his/her children. (11)

9. Agree to defer whenever practical to the biological parent on disciplinary matters relating to his/her children. (12)

10. Discuss financial and disciplinary matters in private, rather than in the presence of the children. (12, 13)

11. Initiate relationship-building activities with stepchildren, and refrain from assuming a disciplinary role before that relationship is well-established. (14)

12. If relations among family members permit, plan an activity or outing (e.g., dinner, movie, shopping venture) that involves the children from each side of the family. (14, 15)

13. Talk positively and respectfully about ex-partners, especially in front of the children. (16)

14. Accept the view that all members of a combined family need not love one another, but they do need to be cordial and respectful. (17, 18, 19)

6. Have partners discuss how they expect to deal with expenses of children's higher education.

7. Have partners discuss who will pay expenses not covered in the divorce agreement (e.g., music and athletic lessons, team uniforms, camp).

8. Encourage open discussion and guide problem-solving efforts to help parents provide financially and emotionally fair support of the children.

9. Ask partners to make explicit the implicit agreements that have evolved between them and ex-partners (e.g., who is to pick up the children for visitation).

10. If an ex-partner has violated a divorce agreement regarding child support and/or maintenance, have partners discuss how long they will allow the violation to continue before taking some action, such as having the financial matters handled directly by the court.

11. Remind parents that in most states visitation is viewed as a privilege, not a legal responsibility. Have them verbalize the difficulties and pain they may experience about an ex-partner's infrequent or nonexistent visits with child.

15. Encourage children to speak positively of parents' ex-partners (when realistic) by describing some of those positive attributes to the children. (20, 21)

16. Ask children about enjoyable activities they have had with the parents' ex-partner during visitation. (21)

17. Accept view that having to talk with ex-partners is necessary, and agree to not interfere with such communication between other partner and his/her ex-partner. (22)

18. Avoid arguments with ex-partner, especially in front of the children. (23)

__. _____
   _____

__. _____
   _____

__. _____
   _____

12. Solicit agreement from non-biological parent to support biological parent's discipline behaviors and to defer such responsibilities to biological parent whenever practical (especially with children more than 10 years old).

13. Have partners discuss disciplinary and financial matters that generate disagreement. Assign similar discussions for private homework (i.e., not in the presence of the children).

14. Have partners initiate appropriate relationship-building activities with the nonbiological child (for example, bike riding, attending child's sport or musical activities, playing together, talking about child's interests, watching a child's video together).

15. Encourage partners to help each child demonstrate acceptance of his/her new stepmother or stepfather via cordial, respectful, and civil interactions.

16. Encourage partners to avoid blaming their respective ex-partners (and their respective ex-partners' new love interest) for the "dissolution of our family."

17. Remind partners that "instant love" of new family members is a myth. It is unrealistic to expect children to like (and certainly

to love) the partner who is serving in the new-parent role.

18. Help partners accept the position that siblings from different biological families need not like or love one another but should be mutually respectful and kind.

19. If siblings from two different biological families do not get along well, have partners plan separate outings with each set of children.

20. Role-play and model with the partners some of the positive things they can say in front of the children about the positive qualities of an ex-partner.

21. Assign partners to talk with their children about some of the nice things the children experienced during visitation, or vacation, with an ex-partner. Review and discuss these attempts to talk positively about ex-partner.

22. Help partners agree about the need for open communication with ex-partners about matters pertaining to the children.

23. Rehearse with partners ways they can avoid arguments and hostile interactions during problem-solving meetings with their ex-partners.

—. _____
    _____
—. _____
    _____
—. _____
    _____

DIAGNOSIS SUGGESTIONS:

Axis I: V61.20   Parent-Child Relational Problem
           V61.1   Partner Relational Problem
           V61.8   Sibling Relational Problem
           _____   _____
           _____   _____

COMMUNICATION

BEHAVIORAL DEFINITIONS

1. Frequent arguments, or arguing in ways that cause excessive upset.
2. Difficulty in resolving problems.
3. Frequent misunderstandings during discussions.
4. Viewing disagreements as symbols of global problems (e.g., such core themes as love and respect) rather than as specific problems.
5. Consistent failure to verbally acknowledge the positive actions of the other partner.

LONG-TERM GOALS

1. Partners communicate about feelings without discussion escalating into a verbal fight.
2. Partners discuss and resolve problems without verbal fighting.
3. Each partner listens to and understands the other partner's perspective.
4. Arguments no longer feel like uncontrollable, inevitable events, as partners learn to recognize cues of verbal fighting, and control them before they start.

5. Partners recognize and overtly acknowledge when core themes are evoked.
6. Each partner notices and verbalizes appreciation to the other for acts of kindness, thoughtfulness, and caring.

—. _____
  _____
  _____
—. _____
  _____
  _____
—. _____
  _____

SHORT-TERM OBJECTIVES

1. Verbally contract to identify specific communication deficits. (1, 2, 3)
2. Practice defining problems in specific, nonblaming terms. (4, 5, 6)
3. Practice listening in a manner that promotes empathy and understanding. (7, 8, 9, 10)
4. Practice sharing thoughts and feelings in a manner that promotes intimacy. (11, 12)
5. Identify the current purpose of the conversation (i.e., venting or problem solving) when serving as either the speaker or listener. (13, 14)
6. Practice accepting and rejecting requests for positive activities. (15, 16)
7. Set aside 10 to 15 minutes several times per week for

THERAPEUTIC INTERVENTIONS

1. Have the couple attempt to solve a major problem while the therapist quietly watches and takes notes about communication skills and deficits.
2. Positively reinforce the couple about things they do well (such as making eye contact or attempting to define the problem) and provide direct feedback regarding things that need improvement (such as maintaining a civil tone of voice or overcoming tendency to interrupt).
3. Ask partners to list (a) actions each can take to help solve communication problems and (b) actions that tend to make matters worse.
4. Have partners take turns "pinpointing" problems

discussion of personal issues. (17)

8. Demonstrate de-escalating conflict. (18, 19, 20, 21)

9. Identify cues for arguments and practice argument-control strategies. (22, 23, 24)

10. List the cues that each partner will use to judge that the other is receptive to problem solving at a specific time. (25)

11. Verbalize how a problem may be opened for discussion. (26, 27)

12. Demonstrate harmony in defining the exact nature of a problem before trying to resolve it. (28)

13. Agree to discuss only one problem at a time after it has been pinpointed. (29)

14. Agree to use a brainstorming technique as one problem-solving approach. (30, 31, 32)

15. Identify core themes of fights and overtly communicate about them. (33, 34)

16. Attend to and compliment other partner for helpful or caring behaviors. (35, 36)

__. _____
   _____

__. _____
   _____

__. _____
   _____

(that is, making requests for change that are specific, observable, and ask for increases rather than decreases in the other partner's behavior).

5. Have partners role-play at making "I" statements in the following form: "When _____ happens, I feel _____. I would like _____."

6. If either partner is mind-reading the other, have him/her rephrase statements so that he/she is speaking only for self and expressing own perceptions.

7. While one partner is serving as the speaker, have the other paraphrase, by repeating back in his/her own words, the speaker's overt point (e.g., "You would like me to balance the checkbook with you each month").

8. While one partner is serving as the speaker, have the other reflect, by repeating back in his/her own words, the speaker's underlying emotion (e.g., "You're frustrated about our inability to save money").

9. Have the listening partner practice validation skills (i.e., the listener conveys that he/she understands and can empathize with the speaker's feelings, even if not agreeing with them).

10. If understanding or problem solving is at an impasse, have partners switch places and discuss the issue from the other's perspective.

11. Have partners share their feelings regarding issues about which they'd like to be closer. Provide a list of "emotion" words, if necessary, to cue partners to the subtleties of words expressing feelings.

12. Teach partners the speaker skill of "measured truthfulness" (i.e., balancing the need to comment about the partner, against a concern for his/her feelings), and have them practice this on areas of conflict.

13. Teach partners that communication tends to serve one of two purposes—venting (i.e., sharing feelings) or problem solving. Have partners identify how they feel when one person is pursuing venting and the other problem solving.

14. Role-play at having the listener ask the speaker which he/she wants out of the discussion—venting or problem solving.

15. Have one partner practice making suggestions for enjoyable activities together and the other practice accepting (by making eye contact, reinforcing the person for asking, and

planning when to do the activity).

16. Have one partner practice making suggestions for enjoyable activities together and the other practice rejecting using the positive-negative-positive "sandwich" method (reinforcing the partner for asking, identifying the specific element being rejected, and making a counter-suggestion).

17. Assign the partners to set aside 10 to 15 minutes two or three times a week for a "couple meeting," to discuss suggestions and/or complaints in a constructive manner.

18. Teach partners the listener skill of "editing" (i.e., responding to provocation in a manner that is in one's long-term best interest, rather than for retaliation or debate) and have them practice this on areas of conflict.

19. Teach partners the listener skill of "metacommunication" (i.e., commenting on the *process* rather than the *content* of the speaker's statement) and have them practice this to overtly correct dysfunctional communication, rather than acting out of anger over negative communication behaviors.

20. Ask each partner to identify behaviors that he/she

employs during discussions to (*a*) soothe him/herself or the other partner, or (*b*) de-escalate the conflict.

21. Ask each partner to confirm whether he/she interprets the other's supposed soothing/de-escalation behaviors as such. If so, ask for future increases in soothing/de-escalation. If not, have partners discuss their opposing interpretations of the behavior.

22. Help partners identify cues that an argument is impending (e.g., behaviors, thoughts, feelings, bodily sensations) and have them contract with each other actions they will take to cool off before talking further.

23. Assign partners to track times and places that trigger arguments.

24. Help partners identify times that are conducive to discussing and/or solving problems (such as after the children are in bed) and times that are not conducive (such as when dinner is being prepared).

25. Help partners identify the cues that indicate that either is receptive to discussing and/or solving problems (for example, partner is awake, alert, and not too tired; no distractions are present; no alcohol has been consumed; and enough time

is available for attaining closure).

26. Have each partner practice approaching the other to discuss a problem.

27. Have both partners agree on an agenda and time limit for problem-solving discussions.

28. Teach partners to agree to their mutual satisfaction that a problem has been correctly pinpointed, before actually trying to solve the problem. Have them practice this in session on areas of conflict.

29. Have both partners agree to discuss one problem only during problem-solving discussions.

30. Model a brainstorming technique that produces at least two solutions to a problem before trying to solve that problem. Have the partners practice this in session on areas of conflict.

31. Teach partners to evaluate the pros and cons of the brainstormed solutions and have them practice this in session on areas of conflict.

32. Teach partners how to make a specific, pinpointed plan for attaining a solution. Have the plan include a time in the future to evaluate progress on the solution. Have the partners practice this in session on areas of conflict.

33. Help partners identify the core themes (e.g., love, respect, power differentials) that underlie their most effectively charged arguments.

34. Have partners practice overtly discussing the core theme as part of their problem discussions.

35. Assign both partners to track on paper and bring to session the "Catch your partner pleasing you" exercise. Note (*a*) at least one positive behavior they noticed the partner do each day; and (*b*) at least one positive behavior they did themselves that day.

36. Have each partner use "I" statements to express his/her appreciation for the other partner's behaviors noted on the "catch your partner pleasing you" tracking sheet.

___. _____
    _____
___. _____
    _____
___. _____
    _____

DIAGNOSIS SUGGESTIONS

| Axis I | 309.24 | Adjustment Disorder With Anxiety |
| | 309.0 | Adjustment Disorder With Depressed Mood |

	309.3	Adjustment Disorders With Disturbance of Conduct
	309.28	Adjustment Disorder With Mixed Anxiety and Depressed Mood
	309.4	Adjustment Disorder With Mixed Disturbance of Emotions and Conduct
	305.00	Alcohol Abuse
	303.90	Alcohol Dependence
	296.x	Bipolar I Disorder
	300.4	Dysthymic Disorder
	296.x	Major Depressive Disorder
	V61.1	Physical Abuse of Adult, 995.81 Victim
	V61.1	Partner Relational Problem
	_____	_____
Axis II	_____	_____
	301.7	Antisocial Personality Disorder
	301.83	Borderline Personality Disorder
	301.50	Histrionic Personality Disorder
	301.81	Narcissistic Personality Disorder
	_____	_____
	_____	_____

DEPENDENCY

BEHAVIORAL DEFINITIONS

1. Derives self-worth almost solely from positive partner comments, leading to incessant solicitation of feedback.
2. Fears being abandoned by partner.
3. Has difficulty making decisions without confirmation by or support of partner.
4. Avoids expressing disagreement with partner because of fear of disapproval or rejection.
5. Assumes a servant role with partner, doing almost anything to gain approval.
6. Has a history of going from one relationship to another with little time between relationships.
7. Initiates contact with partner in diverse settings (e.g., when partner is at work, driving, or at gym) because of need for reassurance and fear of being alone.
8. Jealous of time partner spends with work colleagues and suspected sexual partners.
9. Feels anxious if partner is not available for support or encouragement.

—. _____

_____

—. _____

_____

—. _____

_____

LONG-TERM GOALS

1. Increase self-esteem and self-confidence, leading to efficient decision-making, greater tolerance for being alone, and a sense of secure independence.
2. Accepts legitimate absences of partner (such as being at work) without anxiety.
3. Contacts partner only when necessary if partner is at work or engaged in a recreational activity.
4. Makes routine decisions independently (i.e., without partner).
5. Accepts the need for partner to spend time with colleagues and friends.
6. Broadens sources of self-worth (i.e., not just the partner).

—. _____

_____

—. _____

_____

—. _____

_____

SHORT-TERM OBJECTIVES

1. Dependent partner, acknowledge that he/she has contacted partner excessively when partner had a right to be alone or to conduct personal activities without intrusion. (1, 2, 29)
2. Read the book *Co-Dependent No More* and then identify how he/she is demonstrating dependent behaviors in relationship with other partner. (3, 4, 6)
3. Identify behavioral goals that will be incompatible with continuing the dependency patterns that are

THERAPEUTIC INTERVENTIONS

1. Ask dependent partner to list the situations that lead to anxiety such that he/she contacts the other partner unnecessarily.
2. Have nondependent partner provide feedback about how the intrusiveness of dependent partner affects him/her.
3. Assign dependent partner to read *Co-Dependent No More* (Beattie).
4. Discuss *Co-Dependent No More* in conjoint session and have dependent partner

causing conflict in the relationship. (5)

4. Dependent partner, identify those areas of other partner's life that should not be intruded upon, and pledge to provide privacy. (5, 6, 29)

5. Describe interactions with other partner that demonstrate a change from dependency behaviors to independence, self-confidence, and freedom from fear of rejection or disapproval. (7, 30)

6. Describe instances where the other (dependent) partner has disagreed with, been comfortable being separated from, and/or asked nondependent partner for a sacrificial favor. (7, 8, 18, 29, 30)

7. Nondependent partner, report instances of providing positive reinforcement to other partner on occasions when he/she has not sought reassurance or intruded upon partner's privacy. (8)

8. Nondependent partner, offer reassurance, compliments, and expressions of appreciation to other partner on a regular basis, without being prompted. (9)

9. Dependent partner, report instances of feeling more comfortable in the face of other partner's criticism and not fearful of that rejec-

identify his/her dependent patterns.

5. Assist dependent partner in setting graduated behavioral goals for increasing independence in the relationship.

6. Ask dependent partner to list the boundaries that he/she crossed in the last week with partner.

7. Have dependent partner describe to other partner how he/she is becoming less dependent.

8. Have nondependent partner provide feedback to other partner about progress that is being made in observing boundaries.

9. Encourage nondependent partner to tell partner noncontingently that he/she cares for him/her (i.e., give reassurance only when dependent partner is not asking for it).

10. Explore and resolve dependent partner's fear of rejection that originates in lack of acceptance from family of origin. Help him/her separate the early fear and anger from current relationship.

11. Discuss in conjoint session how both independence and dependence can be positive for relationship (e.g., encourages mutual respect for personal traits and

tion or overly defensive. (10, 29, 30)

10. Dependent partner, list ways that a healthy inter-dependence with other part-ner can be demonstrated, as differentiated from total emotional dependence. (11)

11. Dependent partner, state the boundaries needed for self in relationships. (12, 29)

12. Dependent partner, list other relationships that have similar patterns of fear of abandonment, need for constant reassurance, and a persistent attempt to please. (13, 29)

13. Acknowledge and report instances of imposing self on people other than part-ner because of the strong need for reassurance and fear of being alone. (13, 14, 29)

14. Describe interactions with friends, coworkers, or extended family that fit the pattern of being indecisive, fearing disapproval, or being too eager to please. (15, 29, 30)

15. Verbalize the benefits of not imposing fears, needs, and private thoughts on others. (16)

16. Acknowledge that pattern of insecurity, eagerness to please, and low self-esteem in relationships goes beyond the present relation-ship and has roots in the

abilities, allows *each* partner to give support to the other).

12. Have dependent partner list what boundary behaviors he/she must instill into non-intimate relationships (such as keeping certain thoughts and feelings private, allow-ing others privacy and time alone, and making personal decisions without anxiety or seeking approval).

13. Have dependent partner discuss whether boundary issues are restricted to the other partner or are gener-alized (i.e., occur with coworkers, other family members).

14. Ask dependent partner to list any boundaries that he/she crossed during the last week with coworkers and/or family members.

15. Help dependent partner understand how fear of rejection or disapproval influences relationships with others beyond nonde-pendent partner. Encourage confidence and assertive-ness.

16. Assist dependent partner in listing the benefits of being more private in casual rela-tionships (e.g., less alien-ation of self from others, more pride and respect for self, projects image of more competence and less needi-ness).

family of origin. (10, 17, 29)

17. Identify interactions in family of origin that created fear of trusting relationships as reliable or self as loveable. (10, 17, 18)

18. Both partners identify sources of emotional support outside of the other partner and list five reasons why social support outside the relationship is good for the relationship. (19)

19. List three reasons why affirmation from others outside the relationship is good for building self-esteem. (19)

20. Dependent partner, identify how being an independent person is good both for one's self-esteem and for the relationship. (20)

21. Dependent partner, report instances with friends or family of asserting self, asking for something for self, and/or accepting criticism or disapproval without anxiety. (21, 30)

22. Dependent partner, report increasingly greater amounts of time spent away from partner, doing daily routine duties without initiating contact and without worry. (22, 23, 30)

23. Dependent partner, take an overnight trip alone to visit a friend or family member. (22, 23, 30)

24. Dependent partner, list

17. Have both partners discuss their dependency patterns in their families of origin.

18. Explore abandonment experiences in family of origin and with significant others in adulthood (i.e., past events that could be fueling the current fears of abandonment).

19. Discuss how support from others outside the relationship can actually benefit the relationship (e.g., decreases the need for partner support, broadens social support network, affirms self in ways that cannot or will not be satisfied by partner).

20. Encourage dependent partner to set goals for independence and to discuss how independence builds self-esteem and makes a relationship more interesting.

21. Reinforce dependent partner's reports of progress in independence, decision making, assertiveness, and resilience in the face of disapproval.

22. Encourage dependent partner to take increasingly larger ventures on own (e.g., to store, gym, social outing, overnight trips).

23. Assign dependent partner to increase time spent at work or play without partner contact.

decisions made without consulting others for reassurance or agreement. (24, 25)

25. List the legitimate needs that each partner can expect the other to fulfill. (26, 28)

26. List the legitimate rights that each partner has within the relationship. (26, 28)

27. List the legitimate rights that each partner has in relationships with others (e.g., coworkers or family). (27, 28)

28. Verbalize negative automatic thoughts associated with assertiveness, being alone, or refusing to meet others' needs. (29)

29. Using role-playing, practice replacing negative thoughts with healthy, positive self-talk. (30)

30. Attend assertiveness-training class to learn ways to get own needs met in a healthy, direct manner and to say no without guilt or fear of rejection. (31)

__. _____
_____

__. _____
_____

__. _____
_____

24. Encourage dependent partner to make decisions on his/her own (i.e., without input from other partner).

25. Have nondependent partner provide positive feedback about good decisions made unilaterally by dependent partner.

26. Ask each partner to list the legitimate rights that he/she has, and needs that could be fulfilled by the other partner.

27. Ask each partner to list the legitimate rights that others have in relationship, and needs that could be fulfilled by family or coworkers.

28. Discuss the rights and needs of each partner that can impact relationships with partner and others.

29. Explore dependent client's automatic thoughts associated with assertiveness, being alone, or not meeting others' needs.

30. Through modeling, assist dependent partner in developing positive self-talk to replace negative thoughts that precipitate fear and desperation.

31. Refer dependent partner to assertiveness-training classes.

__. _____
_____

—. _____
_____

—. _____
_____

DIAGNOSTIC SUGGESTIONS

Axis I:	311	Depressive Disorder NOS
	300.4	Dysthymic Disorder
	296.xx	Major Depressive Episode
	_____	_____
	_____	_____
Axis II:	301.6	Dependent Personality Disorder
	301.82	Avoidant Personality Disorder
	_____	_____
	_____	_____

DEPRESSION INDEPENDENT OF RELATIONSHIP PROBLEMS

BEHAVIORAL DEFINITIONS

1. Pervasive feeling of sadness and dissatisfaction with life.
2. Difficulties in concentrating.
3. Lack of interest in sexual interactions.
4. Difficulty in sleeping, or sleeping too much.
5. Lack of energy.
6. Withdrawal from social activities.
7. Low self-esteem or feelings of worthlessness.
8. Feelings of hopelessness.
9. Suicidal thoughts and/or behavior.
10. Feelings of guilt, especially because of relationship problems related to the depression.
11. Movement retardation or acceleration (slowed activity or pacing).
12. Chronic or recurrent feelings of depression.
13. Lack of responsiveness to antidepressant medication.
14. Responsive to antidepressant medication, but chooses not to take such medication due to side effects.
15. Unable to resolve grief.

Partner-assisted therapy has been used successfully both in Europe and the United States, but there is no particular protocol for such therapy. However, a sensitive, empathetic partner can be of great value in partner-assisted therapy for depression. On the other hand, a partner who is prone to being critical can undermine therapy, even if the overall relationship is satisfactory. Thus, a careful, accurate assessment of the potential for support or harm by the partner's participation in some or all of the therapy sessions is crucial to the success of the therapy.

—. _____

_____

—. _____

_____

—. _____

_____

LONG-TERM GOALS

1. Reduce depression and increase energy level.
2. Increase self-esteem.
3. Recognize why grief is prolonged; resolve grief; and return to normal, nondepressed functioning.
4. Recognize factors that have led to depression and cope with them in a manner that makes relapse less likely.
5. Develop positive attitudes and beliefs that make relapse less likely.
6. Capitalize on the support and positive feedback of partner and understanding of depression to increase self-esteem and make relapse less likely.

—. _____

_____

—. _____

_____

—. _____

_____

SHORT-TERM OBJECTIVES

1. Identify sources of depressed mood and related depressive symptoms. (1, 2, 9)

2. List changes that could be made in causative factors or own attitude (or self-talk

THERAPEUTIC INTERVENTIONS

1. Ask client to list all the factors that seem to make him/her depressed.

2. Have client rank in order of importance the factors that are making him/her depressed.

messages) that could result in improved mood. (3)

3. Complete standardized measures of depression and suicidal ideation, and process feedback about the results. (4)

4. Verbally understand and agree upon a plan of preventative action to be used if suicidal thoughts become frequent and intense. (5)

5. Identify possible genetic and family-of-origin factors that relate to a vulnerability to depression. (6, 7)

6. Describe instances of verbalized anger toward other partner for his/her perceived lack of support or withdrawal during a depressive episode. (8)

7. Verbalize a plan for appropriate sharing of depressed feelings with family and friends (while being careful to not alienate self from others by constant negativity). (9, 10)

8. Use prayer, meditation, and/or attendance at religious services when such seems to have provided benefit in the past for alleviation of feelings of hopelessness or worthlessness. (11)

9. Take antidepressant medication as prescribed by physician. (12, 13)

3. Explore changes that can be made in causative factors, or in client's negative interpretation of them, that could result in improved mood.

4. Administer standardized measures of depression and hopelessness (e.g., Beck Depression Inventory, Beck Hopelessness Inventory) and review results with client.

5. Develop plan of action with client about whom to call if hopeless feelings are becoming magnified, and arrange for 24-hour coverage at these times with clear instructions how to reach help.

6. Assign client to make a family tree with brief descriptions of mental health of each family member and notations whether they experienced depression.

7. Discuss family risk and genetic liability for depression, but emphasize the equally important roles that psychological and environmental factors play in preventing and coping with depression even when hereditary risk factors are high.

8. Discuss how individuals with depression often become angry quickly and make hostile comments to

10. Report side effects and effectiveness of medication to physician. (13, 14)

11. Verbalize a willingness to cooperate with alternatives to the particular antidepressant medication, if not responsive to the medication. (15, 16)

12. Engage in some daily activity (i.e., visiting or phoning a friend) that requires taking care of one's appearance and involves interactions with others. (17)

13. When possible, use support of partner through phone contact during day. (18)

14. Engage in physical activity (walk, jog, work out in gym, ride bicycle) to help overcome depressed feelings. (19)

15. Report instances of making positive statements to self and others about the future. (20)

16. Partner without depression, avoid taking other partner's depression or aversive behaviors personally. (21)

17. Partner without depression, hold realistic expectations for other partner's functioning. (22)

18. Read *Feeling Good* to better understand and cope with depression. (23)

—. _____

_____

people they love. Encourage client to monitor self and minimize such hostile comments.

9. Encourage sharing of depressed feelings in therapy session and, on a limited basis, with significant others, to help them understand the factors that lead to depression.

10. Have client verbally outline appropriate reliance on significant others (friends and family) to minimize avoidance of the client by friends.

11. Encourage use of religious services, spiritual writings, and prayer if these have proven useful in the past, and/or if client seems desirous of beginning such endeavors.

12. When antidepressant medication appears to be called for, make referral to psychiatrist or other physician for medication, and encourage client to take medication regularly.

13. Educate client on the common side effects of various antidepressant medications (such as nausea, anxiety and nervousness, insomnia, dry mouth, or decreased sexual arousal), but note that these often go away during the first few weeks of medication.

__. _____
    _____
__. _____
    _____

14. Have client report side effects and effectiveness of medications to physician.

15. If client is unresponsive to antidepressant medication, have him/her discuss lack of responsiveness with physician and raise the issue of changing dosage and/or medication.

16. If client is unresponsive to other medications, discuss the option of electroconvulsive shock therapy. Review the positive effects that such treatments have had on patients who have been unresponsive to antidepressants.

17. Assign client to make a certain number of social contacts (phone calls, visits, letter-writing, e-mail) per week.

18. Assign client to make a certain number of contacts with other partner per week at his/her work, provided that such contacts are permitted by the employer, and the partner is supportive.

19. Assist client in planning regular physical activities (e.g., walking, jogging, working out in gym). When appropriate, involve partner in these activities.

20. Encourage client to engage in positive self-talk. Reinforce verbalizations of hope- and self-esteem-enhancing thoughts.

21. Educate partner without depression that other partner's mood and aversive behaviors are symptomatic of clinical depression.

22. Encourage partner without depression to adjust expectations to the severity of the partner's depression-impaired functioning.

23. Assign client to read *Feeling Good* (Burns, 1980).

__. _____
    _____

__. _____
    _____

__. _____
    _____

DIAGNOSTIC SUGGESTIONS

Axis I: 309.0   Adjustment Disorder With Depressed Mood
            V62.82   Bereavement
            300.4   Dysthymic Disorder
            296.xx   Major Depressive Episode
            _____   _____
            _____   _____

Axis II: 301.83   Borderline Personality Disorder
            _____   _____
            _____   _____

DEPRESSION DUE TO RELATIONSHIP PROBLEMS

BEHAVIORAL DEFINITIONS

1. Feeling blue.
2. Difficulties in concentrating.
3. Lack of interest in sexual interactions.
4. Difficulty in sleeping, or sleeping too much.
5. Lack of energy.
6. Withdrawal from social activities.
7. Low self-esteem.
8. Feelings of hopelessness.
9. Suicidal thoughts and/or behavior.
10. Feelings of guilt, especially because of relationship problems related to the depression.
11. Movement retardation or acceleration (slowed activity or pacing).
12. Recurrent crying spells.
13. Lack of responsiveness to antidepressant medication.
14. Responsive to antidepressant medication, but chooses not to take such medication due to side effects.
15. Inability to resolve grief.
16. Belief that relationship problems are the cause of depression.
17. History of relationship problems prior to the depression.
18. History of some precipitating event in the relationship that was very destructive (e.g., verbal abuse, physical abuse, discovery of action by other partner that led to distrust).

—. _____

_____

—. _____

_____

—. _____

_____

LONG-TERM GOALS

1. Increase partners' general level of satisfaction with relationship.
2. Reduce client's depressed mood and increase his/her energy level.
3. Increase client's self-esteem.
4. Recognize factors that led to client's depressed feelings and cope with them in a manner that makes relapse less likely.

—. _____

_____

—. _____

_____

—. _____

_____

SHORT-TERM OBJECTIVES

1. Describe overall level of satisfaction with the relationship. (1)
2. Complete relationship assessment instruments. (2)
3. Verbalize own level of commitment to remain in the relationship. (3)
4. Describe extent of own love and caring for the other partner. (4)
5. Identify sources of depressed mood and related depressive symptoms, focusing on the role of conflicts

THERAPEUTIC INTERVENTIONS

1. Explore each partner's thoughts and feelings concerning the relationship.
2. Have each partner complete some standardized assessment of relationship satisfaction (e.g., Locke Wallace Marital Adjustment Test, 1959, or Spanier Dyadic Adjustment Scale, 1976).
3. Have each partner describe his/her commitment to the relationship and/or complete a standardized commitment to relationship

within the relationship. (5, 6, 7)

6. Complete standardized measures of depression and suicidal ideation. (8)

7. Implement a plan of preventative action to be used if suicidal thoughts become frequent. (9)

8. Verbalize an understanding of how anger and depression interact. (10)

9. Reduce the frequency of critical, angry expressions that are related to general state of depression. (11)

10. Describe instances of sharing depressed feelings in a controlled, limited manner that is sensitive to not alienating self from others. (12, 13)

11. Use prayer, meditation, and/or attendance at religious services if doing so seems to have provided benefit in the past. (14)

12. Apologize and offer restitution to other partner for past nonsupportive behavior. (15)

13. Describe instances of positive, supportive comments being given to each other. (16)

14. Engage in positive interaction with other partner. (15, 16, 17)

15. Describe instances of verbal and physical affection

scale (e.g., Commitment Scale by Broderick and O'Leary, 1986).

4. Have each partner articulate and/or complete an assessment of love/caring for the other partner (e.g., Positive Feelings Questionnaire; see O'Leary, 1987).

5. Assess the extent to which each partner believes relationship problems preceded the depression.

6. Have each partner describe whether and why he/she believes the depression was caused by problems in the relationship.

7. Have client rank in order of importance all the factors that are making him/her depressed.

8. Administer standardized measures of depression and hopelessness (such as Beck Depression Inventory or Beck Hopelessness Scale) and provide feedback on the results.

9. Develop plan of action with client about whom to call if hopeless feelings are becoming magnified, and arrange for 24-hour coverage with clear instructions to client about how to reach help.

10. Teach how individuals with depression often become angry quickly and make hostile comments to people they love.

between self and other partner. (18)

16. Reduce frequency of hostile comments related to dissatisfaction with other partner. (10, 11, 19, 20)

17. As a means of increasing awareness, identify instances of self issuing negative, hostile comments. (21, 22)

18. Cooperate with a medication evaluation by a physician. (23)

19. Take prescribed antidepressant medication at times ordered by physician and report therapeutic impact and any side effects. (24, 25)

20. Verbalize an understanding of alternatives to the particular antidepressant medication being used (dose and alternative medications), if unresponsive to the medication. (26)

21. Verbalize an awareness of the frequency with which critical, hopeless, and pessimistic self-talk is engaged in. (27, 28)

22. Make positive statements to self and others about the future. (28, 29)

___. _____
   _____
___. _____
   _____
___. _____
   _____

11. Ask client with depression to monitor self and minimize hostile comments to other partner.

12. Encourage sharing of depressed feelings in therapy session and, on a limited basis, with significant others.

13. Have client verbally outline appropriate reliance on significant others (friends and family) to minimize avoidance of the client by friends.

14. Encourage use of religious services, spiritual writings, and prayer if those have proven useful in the past and/or if client seems desirous of beginning such endeavors.

15. Encourage partner who has been nonsupportive to apologize and make some restitution for lack of support.

16. Assign each partner to give positive, supportive comments to the other on a daily basis.

17. Help clients list thoughtful, kind acts that each partner would appreciate and then assign each to engage in at least one caring gesture toward the other each day.

18. If the level of anger and hostility has subsided, assign partners to be verbally and physically affectionate to each other each day.

19. Have partner without depression refrain from making hostile, counter-

productive comments to other partner out of frustration with his/her depression.

20. Provide feedback to both partners regarding the extent of negativity and hostility that exists in their communication.

21. If therapist's requests to avoid negativity prove ineffective, provide audio or videotaped feedback to illustrate the hostility displayed in the session.

22. If therapist's request to avoid negativity prove ineffective, encourage adjunctive individual sessions to address the anger and hostility.

23. If the relationship problems have subsided but the depression has not, refer client with depression to psychiatrist or other physician for medication.

24. Encourage client with depression to take medication regularly and monitor for side effects and effectiveness.

25. Educate the client on the common and often expected side effects of various antidepressant medications (such as nausea, anxiety and nervousness, insomnia, dry mouth, or diminished sexual arousal), but note that these often go away during the first few weeks of medication.

26. If client is unresponsive to antidepressant medication,

have him/her discuss lack of responsiveness with physician and raise the issue of changing dosage and/or medication.

27. If client continues to engage in pessimistic self-talk regarding self, partner, and the future, confront and highlight these negative expressions.

28. Teach client to replace negative self-talk with positive messages regarding self, partner, and future of the relationship.

29. Reinforce client's verbalizations of hope and self-esteem-enhancing thoughts.

___. _____
   _____

___. _____
   _____

___. _____
   _____

DIAGNOSTIC SUGGESTIONS

Axis I:	309.0	Adjustment Disorder With Depressed Mood
	V62.82	Bereavement
	300.4	Dysthymic Disorder
	296.xx	Major Depressive Episode
	V61.1	Physical Abuse of Adult, 995.81 Adult
	V61.1	Partner Relational Problem
	_____	_____
	_____	_____
Axis II:	301.83	Borderline Personality Disorder
	_____	_____
	_____	_____

DISILLUSIONMENT WITH RELATIONSHIP

BEHAVIORAL DEFINITIONS

1. Increasing feelings of being "out of touch" with other partner (i.e., distant, detached, and/or resentful).
2. Trend toward going own way in life, with decreasing sharing of activities, interests, and communication between self and other partner.
3. Fears by one or both partners that relationship will deteriorate to the point of separation or divorce.
4. Arguments or distance created by failed attempts to jointly attend to needs of relationship.
5. Blaming other partner for past personal and relationship disappointments.
6. Difficulty in planning for the future because of arguments or distance in the relationship.
7. Expectations of the self, partner, and/or relationship that lead to negative outcomes (e.g., frustrations, disappointments, depression, anxiety, anger).
8. Increasing preoccupation with past personal and relationship disappointments.

—. _____
   _____
—. _____
   _____
—. _____
   _____

LONG-TERM GOALS

1. Partners rededicate selves to meeting each other's needs and attending to each other's interests.
2. Partners recognize pros and cons of current relationship and commit to actively building on the positive aspects of that relationship.
3. Renegotiate the relationship contract to increase its helpfulness for current coping needs.
4. Commit to improve coping by working together as a team.

__. _____
_____
__. _____
_____
__. _____
_____

SHORT-TERM OBJECTIVES

1. Each partner identify own attitude about making changes to resolve the relationship dissatisfaction. (1)
2. List the current strengths and weaknesses of the relationship. (2, 3)
3. Each partner list three changes he/she will make to improve the relationship. (4)
4. Identify the ways in which each partner's individual and relationship developmental history may be impacting current functioning. (5, 6)
5. Elucidate the original relationship contract, including both explicit and implicit expectations. (7, 8)

THERAPEUTIC INTERVENTIONS

1. Administer "Stages of Change" questionnaire (Prochaska, et al., 1994) to determine which of the four stages of change (precontemplation, contemplation, action, maintenance) best describes each partner's current approach to the relationship dissatisfaction. Discuss the results in conjoint session.
2. Ask both partners to describe the strengths of their current relationship.
3. Ask both partners to describe the elements of their current relationship that they would like to improve.

6. Verbalize the pros and cons of the original relationship contract. (9, 10)

7. Agree to discard the explicit or implicit expectations in the relationship that have led to conflict, disappointment, or frustration. (11)

8. Identify the ways in which the relationship contract either evolved or needed to evolve but didn't. (12, 13)

9. Each partner state the ways in which his/her personal and relationship dreams have been fulfilled and dashed. (14, 15)

10. Express gratitude to each other for dreams realized, and acceptance or forgiveness for dreams unfulfilled. Agree to no longer hold on to resentment that causes distance in the relationship. (16)

11. Verbalize acceptance of the continuities and disruptions of their lives together by narrating two contrasting versions of their life history. (17, 18)

12. Identify the impact, on both emotions and coping, of viewing their lives as predictable or unpredictable. (19)

13. Identify the security of viewing their life story as predictable and the excitement and need for each other that accompanies life as unpredictable. (20, 21)

4. Have each partner list three ways that he/she could change to cause improvement in those elements of the relationship that he/she would like to improve.

5. Have partners trace important events in their individual developmental that may relate to their current style of interacting.

6. Have partners trace important events in their relationship developmental that may relate to their current style of interacting.

7. Ask partners to describe what their stated expectations were of each other (i.e., the explicit relationship contract).

8. Ask partners to describe what their unspoken expectations were of each other (i.e., the implicit relationship contract).

9. Explore the ways in which the original relationship contract (both implicit and explicit) has benefitted each partner.

10. Explore the negative aspects in the partners' original relationship contract that have led to conflict, disappointment, or frustration.

11. Encourage agreement to eliminate expectations that have been sources of conflict, disappointment, or frustration.

14. Accept responsibility for disappointing decisions by recognizing that they reflected the best that each could do at the time, giving up a pattern of blame of the partner. (22, 23)

15. State an understanding of some current problems as an unintended by-product of individual attempts at coping with life's circumstances. (24, 26)

16. Elucidate the stressful life circumstances over the years that have necessitated coping. (25)

17. Verbalize empathy with the other partner's attempts to cope, and describe the negative impact the partner's coping has had on oneself. (26, 27, 28)

18. Agree to begin to coordinate coping with life's stressors "as a team." (29, 30)

19. Report on recent improvements in communication. (31)

20. State a willingness to redefine relationship roles and expectations. (32)

21. Write a new relationship contract to redefine relationship roles and expectations. (32)

22. Using the new relationship contract to guide the discussion, strategize about meeting future challenges. (32)

23. Identify current needs and resources. (33, 34)

12. Explore how the partners' relationship contract has evolved across time.

13. Explore the ways that the partners' relationship contract needed to change but never did change.

14. Have each partner identify his/her personal dreams, and discuss the ways in which they have been fulfilled and ways in which they have remained unfulfilled.

15. Ask partners to identify the dreams they had for their relationship, and discuss the ways in which these have been fulfilled and ways in which they have remained unfulfilled.

16. Explore the need for partners to express gratitude to each other for dreams that were realized and to let go of resentment over dreams that remained unfulfilled.

17. Have partners tell their life story together, emphasizing the predictability and continuities of their shared life.

18. Have partners retell their life story, emphasizing the surprises, choices, sacrifices, and unpredictability of their shared life.

19. Help the partners compare and contrast the two versions of their past lives and relationship, emphasizing the impact their emotional

24. Catalog needs that will be met within the relationship and those that will be met outside the relationship. (35)

25. Identify support systems that already exist that could be used to assist in the renewal of the relationship. (39)

26. Identify support systems that could be added to assist in the renewal of the relationship. (39)

—. _____
    _____

—. _____
    _____

—. _____
    _____

and coping responses have on the two versions.

20. Have the partners add chapters to each version of their life story, envisioning their future.

21. Help the partners discuss the pros and cons of both versions of their future chapters, emphasizing the security of predictability and the need for each other during times of unpredictability.

22. Reframe past decisions that led to disappointments as being the best decisions that could be made, considering contextual factors that influenced the choices.

23. Have each partner take personal responsibility for disappointing decisions, thereby reducing blame of the other partner.

24. Reframe current problems as a natural outgrowth of the partners' individual attempts to cope with changes forced on them by life's circumstances.

25. Foster acceptance of each other by having partners discuss the life circumstances that have forced them to cope (e.g., changing social expectations, changing gender roles, family life-cycle changes).

26. Foster acceptance of each other by having partners discuss how their individual

attempts to cope with life's stressors have led to current difficulties.

27. Ask listening partner to empathize with speaker's point of view regarding coping.

28. After listener has empathized, have him/her explain the impact the speaker's coping had, and how it forced him/her to cope with speaker's coping attempt.

29. Reframe current problems as resulting from partners being out-of-sync with each other in coping.

30. Help partners agree to begin working on coping "as a team" to get more in sync.

31. Remediate communication problems, as necessary, with interventions from the Communication section of this *Planner*.

32. Have partners hold a "constitutional convention" to re-evaluate their relationship contract, specifying what expectations, rights, and responsibilities each agrees to.

33. Have both partners identify their current needs.

34. Have both partners identify what each is willing to give to the relationship.

35. Have each partner identify the needs that he/she would like to have met within the

relationship, and those that he/she would like to have met outside of the relationship.

36. Ask partners to generate a list of challenges that they anticipate contending with in the future (e.g., retirement, moving, health problems).

37. Using the agreements detailed in the new relationship contract, have couple plan for their future "as a team."

38. Discuss support systems outside of the relationship that are already in place that can help the partners renew the vitality of their relationship (e.g., friends, self-help and support groups, religious community).

39. Discuss support systems outside of the relationship that can be added to help the partners renew the vitality of their relationship (e.g., friends, self-help and support groups, religious community).

__. _____

_____

__. _____

_____

__. _____

_____

DIAGNOSIS SUGGESTIONS

Axis I	309.0	Adjustment Disorder With Depressed Mood
	305.00	Alcohol Abuse
	303.90	Alcohol Dependence
	300.4	Dysthymic Disorder
	296.x	Major Depressive Disorder
	_____	_____
	_____	_____
	V61.1	Partner Relational Problem
Axis II		
	_____	_____
	_____	_____

EATING DISORDER

BEHAVIORAL DEFINITIONS

1. Rapid consumption of large quantities of food in a short time, followed by self-induced vomiting and/or use of laxatives due to fear of weight gain.
2. Extreme weight loss (and amenorrhea in females), with refusal to maintain a minimal healthy weight due to very limited ingestion of food and high frequency of secretive self-induced vomiting, inappropriate use of laxatives, and/or excessive strenuous exercise.
3. Preoccupation with body image related to grossly unrealistic assessment of self as being too fat, or strong denial of recognizing self as emaciated.
4. An irrational fear of becoming overweight.
5. Fluid and electrolyte imbalance due to eating disorder.
6. Avoidance of expressions of affection with partner.
7. Avoidance of sexual interaction with partner.

Clients with eating disorders often have significant relationship problems, and inclusion of the client's partner in a therapeutic endeavor can often be helpful. In fact, the failure to include a partner in some aspect of the treatment, especially if the partner is very critical of the client with an eating disorder, can inadvertently make recovery less likely, since self-esteem problems are so central to eating disorders. On the other hand, the inclusion of a partner in a partner-assisted therapy in no way implies that the partner is responsible for the disorder. In fact, the majority of eating disorders among women start during their teenage years.

As outlined in the DSM-IV, the particular presenting problems vary according to the particular eating disorder, anorexia nervosa or bulimia nervosa. Because this chapter is chiefly concerned with the relationship problems associated with eating disorders, all of the separate presenting problems will not be described here. However, to place the problem in context, the core symptoms

8. Arguments over dieting, binging, and purging.
9. Chronic or recurrent depression (partner with eating disorder).
10. Chronic or recurrent depression (partner without eating disorder).
11. Lack of communication.
12. Intermittently explosive interchanges between partners.

—. _____
   _____
   _____
—. _____
   _____
   _____
—. _____
   _____

LONG-TERM GOALS

1. Increase both partners' understanding of eating disorders.
2. Restore normal eating patterns, body weight, balanced fluid and electrolytes, and realistic perception of body size.
3. Reduce conflict over problems of eating.
4. Increase support of partner without eating disorder for partner with eating disorder.
5. Increase positive communication between partners.
6. Increase expressions of affection between partners.
7. Increase frequency of sexual interactions between partners.

—. _____
   _____

---

common to both anorexia nervosa and bulimia nervosa include (1) exaggerated concern over weight, (2) preoccupation with body image, and (3) unrealistic assessment of self as being overweight. See *DSM-IV* (American Psychiatric Association, 1997) and *The Complete Psychotherapy Treatment Planner, Eating Disorder* (Jongsma and Peterson, 1995) for an elaboration of the presenting problems of eating disorders.

The extent to which the treatment takes place in conjoint sessions, individual sessions, or some combination thereof will vary depending upon the needs of the particular clients. In the assessment phase, individual sessions are most likely, but such sessions could be the predominant mode of treatment with the partner without the eating disorder.

—. _____
_____
_____
—. _____
_____

SHORT-TERM OBJECTIVES

1. Describe the current eating problems of the partner with eating disorder. (1, 2)

2. Identify those factors previous to, outside of, and within the relationship that cause or maintain the eating disorder. (3, 4)

3. Read factual material about prevalence, course, and treatment of eating disorders. (5)

4. Client with eating disorder accept referral to a physician for physical examination. (6)

5. Client without eating disorder verbalize encouragement and appreciation, praise assets, and recognize accomplishments of other partner. (7, 8)

6. Verbalize understanding of risks and potential benefits of appetite-suppressant medication and antidepressant medication to treat eating disorders. (9, 10, 11)

7. Accept referral to a physician for medication evaluation and take any medication ordered. (12)

THERAPEUTIC INTERVENTIONS

1. Ask each client to describe the eating patterns of the partner with eating disorder.

2. Ask partners to describe the purging patterns of the partner with eating disorder.

3. Ask partners to list the factors that they believe are causing the eating problems.

4. Ask partner without eating disorder to list the ways that he/she may be contributing to the exacerbation and/or maintenance of the other partner's eating problems.

5. Assign treatment-related reading to partners (e.g., *Eating Disorders,* brochure #94-3477, NIMH, 1994).

6. Refer partner with eating disorder to a physician to assess physical health and future risks.

7. Educate partners regarding the central role that low self-esteem plays in the development and maintenance of eating disorders.

8. Discuss the need for partner without eating disorder to provide other partner

8. Client without eating disorder identify feelings of anger, concern, and helplessness about other partner's eating disorder. (13)

9. Client with eating disorder verbalize acceptance of responsibility for changing own behavior and for taking responsibility for maintaining a balanced diet. (14)

10. Client without eating disorder commit to avoid monitoring and criticizing other partner's eating (and purging) habits. (15)

11. Identify the specific role that perfectionism plays in relationship and in sexual interaction. (16, 17)

12. Client with eating disorder identify the type of positive feedback most desired from other partner to help build self-esteem. (18)

—. _____
_____

—. _____
_____

—. _____
_____

with supportive feedback to enhance his/her self-esteem.

9. Review current evidence with clients about the role of appetite suppressant medication in treating eating disorders.

10. Review current evidence with clients about the risk involved with use of psychostimulant medication in treating eating disorders.

11. Review current evidence with clients about the role of antidepressant medication in treating eating disorders.

12. Arrange for a medication evaluation and monitor the effectiveness of any psychotropic medication ordered.

13. Have partner without eating disorder describe the ways that he/she experiences conflict and anger over the other partner's eating disorder.

14. Obtain commitment from partner with eating disorder to accept responsibility for changing problematic eating patterns and attitudes.

15. Obtain commitment from partner without eating disorder to minimize attempts to control the eating behavior of the other partner.

16. Discuss with clients the roles that high standards and perfectionism play in

the life of the partner with eating disorder.

17. Review with clients how perfectionism may interfere with various aspects of their relationship, including communication and sexual functioning.

18. Have partner with eating disorder describe in some detail the specific positive feedback that he/she most desires from other partner to help build self-esteem during efforts to overcome eating disorder.

—. _____
    _____
—. _____
    _____
—. _____
    _____

DIAGNOSTIC SUGGESTIONS

Axis I: 303.90   Alcohol Dependence
              305.00   Alcohol Abuse
              307.1   Anorexia Nervosa
              307.51   Bulimia Nervosa
              307.50   Eating Disorder NOS
              296.x   Major Depressive Episode
              V61.1   Partner Relational Problem
              304.80   Polysubstance Dependence
              _____   _____

Axis II: 301.83   Borderline Personality Disorder
              301.6   Dependent Personality Disorder
              _____   _____
              _____   _____

FINANCIAL CONFLICT

BEHAVIORAL DEFINITIONS

1. Arguments over the amount of money spent by one partner.
2. Arguments over how money is spent.
3. Critical comments about partner not making enough money.
4. Arguments over how much money is to be saved.
5. Feelings of being left out of decision-making regarding money.
6. Suspicions that other partner is secretively spending money.
7. Arguments over the need to save money for retirement.
8. Arguments over "legitimate" methods of reporting income for tax purposes.
9. Arguments over the need to shop for the best possible price on an item.

__. _____

_____

__. _____

_____

__. _____

_____

LONG-TERM GOALS

1. Reach mutual agreement regarding the amount of time each partner is expected to be involved in gainful employment.
2. Reduce arguments over how money is spent and how much should be saved.

3. Arrive at long-term financial plans for spending, saving, and investing money.
4. Develop open and honest communication between partners about the budgeting of all money.
5. Accept contrasting opinions regarding the need to work and save money, provided the differences do not adversely affect the family.
6. Address individual problems within the relationship that may interfere with finances (e.g., alcohol dependence, substance abuse, manic depressive disorder, bulimia nervosa, occupational problem).

—. _____
   _____
—. _____
   _____
—. _____
   _____

SHORT-TERM OBJECTIVES

1. Increase awareness of the sources of other partner's anger and disappointment regarding money acquisition and use. (1, 2)
2. Identify and share priorities as to how money should be spent. (3)
3. Identify the differences in priorities that exist between self and other partner. (4)
4. Identify family of origin style of living and use of money, and state their impact on current financial attitudes. (5)
5. Describe the future income, saving, and spending expec-

THERAPEUTIC INTERVENTIONS

1. Ask each partner to describe his/her angry feelings about how money is spent.
2. Ask each partner to describe his/her disappointments regarding money.
3. Have each partner prioritize how money should be spent.
4. Discuss whether there are basic differences over priorities in desired use of money.
5. Have clients describe the use of money in their families of origin and how that history influences their current attitudes about finances.

tations that existed when relationship began. (6)

6. Verbalize whether parents influence current financial decisions. (7)

7. Agree to set financial goals and to make budgetary decisions cooperatively with partner, without undue reaction to family pressure. (8)

8. Practice listening effectively to other partner regarding differing financial ideas and possible solutions to these conflicts. (9, 10, 11, 12)

9. Report on implementing agreed-upon changes in the handling of finances. (13)

10. Verbalize agreement regarding the need for each partner to work. (14, 15, 16)

11. Agree on how a balance will be reached between the need for child care and the need for income production. (17, 18)

12. Agree on steps to begin coping with expenses (and debt-retirement demands) exceeding income. (19)

13. Develop a written plan for current budget and future finances. (20, 21)

14. Verbalize feelings about one partner exercising virtually exclusive control over couple's finances and financial decisions. (22)

6. Ask partners to describe the expectations they had at the beginning of their relationship regarding amount of money they would have.

7. Have each partner explain whether his/her parents influence current financial decisions.

8. Encourage cooperative, partnership-based financial planning that is free from undue family influence.

9. Have each client practice listening without interruption to partner's views about financial and budgetary goals.

10. After partner has listened without interrupting, ask him/her to paraphrase what the other partner said.

11. After paraphrasing and validation, have each partner offer a number of possible solutions to their conflicts about finances while the other partner refrains from interrupting.

12. Have each partner evaluate the other partner's suggested solutions to financial problems.

13. Assign the couple to implement at least one of the possible solutions during the next week.

14. Ask partners to describe their employment situations at the time they first met.

15. Agree on how financial control and decision-making should be shared. (23)

16. Implement a mutual agreement on how to reach decisions regarding the allocation of money. (24)

17. Verbalize conflicts over the issue of control by one partner that goes far beyond finances. (25, 26, 27)

18. State the extent to which any individual behavioral or personality disorder interferes with financial issues in the family. (28, 29)

__. _____
  _____
__. _____
  _____
__. _____
  _____

15. Explore with partners the expectations each had regarding his/her own employment once they were married, and what employment expectations each held for the other.

16. Facilitate agreement between partners regarding current need for each to work versus the value placed on one staying home to manage household and family responsibilities.

17. If the couple has children, have each partner describe what he/she expected in terms of employment for self and other once they had children.

18. Facilitate agreement between partners regarding child-care needs and income needs.

19. Review with partners the need for filing for bankruptcy, applying for welfare, and/or obtaining credit counseling.

20. If financial planning is needed, refer couple to a professional planner (see *Consumer Reports,* 1998, for qualifications of financial planner), or have partners write a current budget and long-range savings and investment plan.

21. If budgeting is a primary need, consult *Family Economics Review,* published by the U.S. Department of

Agriculture (Superinten-
dent of Documents, U.S.
Government Printing
Office, Washington, DC
20402) for information
regarding household
expense allocations.

22. Ask each partner to
describe the ways that
he/she feels controlled by
the other partner.

23. Facilitate agreement
between partners on how
they can cooperatively
make financial decisions,
with each partner's ideas
being respected.

24. Reinforce changes in managing money that reflect
responsible planning, com-
promise, and respectful
cooperation.

25. Assess whether one partner
attempts to restrict the
other in contacts with
family, friends, and/or
enhancement of educa-
tional/vocational skills.

26. If general control of partner
is an issue, consult *Treatment Planner* chapters on
Psychological Abuse and
Physical Abuse.

27. Explore the specific control
that one partner has over
the finances of the partnership and the degree of feeling that other has about it.

28. During individual sessions,
assess whether a personality
or behavioral disorder of
either partner interferes

with financial issues in the family.

29. If assessment reveals that an individual disorder (e.g., alcohol abuse, substance abuse, or occupational problem) interferes with financial solidarity, refer the individual to appropriate services.

___. _____

_____

___. _____

_____

___. _____

_____

DIAGNOSTIC SUGGESTIONS

Axis I:
309.24	Adjustment Disorder With Anxiety
309.0	Adjustment Disorder With Depressed Mood
309.28	Adjustment Disorder With Mixed Anxiety and Depressed Mood
303.90	Alcohol Dependence
305.00	Alcohol Abuse
304.30	Cannabis Dependence
296.0x	Bipolar I Disorder, Single Manic Episode
307.51	Bulimia Nervosa
V62.2	Occupational Problem
V61.1	Partner Relational Problem
_____	_____

Axis II:
301.7	Antisocial Personality Disorder
301.81	Narcissistic Personality Disorder
301.4	Obsessive Compulsive Personality Disorder
301.6	Dependent Personality Disorder
_____	_____
_____	_____

INFIDELITY

BEHAVIORAL DEFINITIONS

1. Sexual behavior (e.g., penile-vaginal intercourse, oral sex, anal sex) that violates the explicit or implicit expectations of the relationship.
2. Nonsexual behavior that involves sharing intimate feelings and thoughts with an extramarital partner, and secrecy that violates the explicit or implicit expectations of the relationship (e.g., secretly sending a dozen roses to an extramarital partner and expressing feelings of romantic attraction; secretly spending a large amount of one-to-one time together in intimate but nonsexual encounters).

—. _____
  _____
—. _____
  _____
—. _____
  _____

LONG-TERM GOALS

1. Partners agree on appropriate emotional, social, and sexual boundaries with others (e.g., acceptable and prohibited behavior).
2. Hurt partner indicates a willingness to attempt to engage in a process of forgiveness and to begin rebuilding a trusting relationship.

3. Unfaithful partner apologizes for his/her decision to engage in the affair and reveals as much about the affair as the hurt partner wants to know in order to start rebuilding a trusting relationship.
4. Partners are able to discuss affair-related individual vulnerabilities and warning signs without defensiveness.
5. Partners recognize and address threats to their relationship.
6. Partners attempt to meet each other's emotional and physical needs.
7. Partners verbally express empathy toward each other and demonstrate shared responsibility for reconstructing the relationship.
8. Through oral and/or written contract, partners explicitly agree on values to be exercised in the reconstructed relationship.
9. If relationship cannot be saved, clients agree to separate and terminate it, but only after a respectful analysis of what led to the breaking of the commitment to faithfulness.

—. _____
  _____
—. _____
  _____
—. _____
  _____

SHORT-TERM OBJECTIVES

1. Verbally commit to: (a) relationship therapy, (b) ambivalence therapy, or (c) separation therapy. (1, 2, 3, 7, 8)

2. Make safety assurances by (a) agreeing not to make threats regarding own safety; (b) agreeing not to make threats about the safety of others; and (c) stop discussing difficult topics at home if either partner believes that the discussion

THERAPEUTIC INTERVENTIONS

1. Establish type of treatment that will be conducted by describing and agreeing on (a) relationship therapy (i.e., the affair will end and the goal will be to salvage the relationship); (b) ambivalence therapy (i.e., the goal will be to clarify the future of the relationship and the affair); or (c) separation therapy (i.e., either client is determined to end the relationship, and

is beginning to escalate out-of-control. (4, 5)

3. Learn more about common reactions to traumatic events by reviewing the symptoms of Major Depressive Disorder and Posttraumatic Stress Disorder. Identify which symptoms the hurt partner is experiencing. (6)

4. Unfaithful partner(s) openly admit to involvement in infidelity. (9)

5. Unfaithful partner verbalize full responsibility for the decision to choose infidelity and apologize directly for the pain caused to other partner, family, and friends. (9)

6. Hurt partner clearly verbalize acceptance of apology from the unfaithful partner for the infidelity and express willingness to begin the process of forgiveness. (10)

7. Unfaithful partner verbally commit to "stop and share technique" (i.e., agree to stop all personal discussions and/or sexual contact with lover and to openly share any future contact without being asked by partner). (11)

8. Discuss the strengths and needs of the relationship and of selves as individuals. (12, 15)

9. Discuss positive shared experiences during early

goal is to separate under the best possible terms).

2. Negotiate "noncollusion contract" with both partners, stipulating that therapist will not agree to secrecy with either, thus establishing therapist's role as working for the mutual well-being of the couple.

3. Contract with clients for specific minimum number of sessions.

4. Have partners contract to avoid deep discussions at home about the affair or future of the relationship during the first month of treatment.

5. Assess for suicidality and homicidality by asking each client individually if they have any thoughts, intent, or means to hurt themselves or others.

6. Normalize hurt partner's experience by giving partners handouts of common reactions to trauma (e.g., symptoms of Major Depressive Disorder and Posttraumatic Stress Disorder) and assessing which symptoms the hurt partner may be experiencing.

7. Provide hope to both partners by assuring them that many relationships do survive infidelity, and that new assumptions can eventually replace shattered ones (i.e., promises of monogamy,

stages of the relationship (e.g., courting, early marriage). (13)

10. Complete "catch your partner pleasing you" exercise at home and bring the list to next session. (12)

11. Identify and list behavioral changes for self and partner that would enhance the relationship. Prioritize the list in order of increasing amount of trust and commitment required for enactment. Process the lists in the next session. (16, 17)

12. Agree to use "time-out" technique to control explosive arguments. (18)

13. Use behavioral rehearsal and role play to assure each other of what each will do if the lover attempts to contact either partner. (19)

14. Learn and give examples of constructive communication skills such as "I" statements and empathic listening. (20)

15. Hurt partner identify facts he/she would like to know about the affair and bring these questions to a session for discussion rather than conduct an inquiry at home. (21)

16. Hurt partner use anxiety management techniques to deal with intrusive thoughts about the affair. (22)

17. Employ communication skills to express hurt and understanding around

trust, honesty, commitment, emotional safety). Assign reading *After The Affair* (Spring) and *Private Lies* (Pittman).

8. Educate partners regarding common course of therapy for infidelity; that is, that progress often also involves emotional setbacks, and that setbacks frequently follow times of increased closeness and vulnerability.

9. Encourage unfaithful partner to accept full responsibility for the decision to engage in affair and to apologize directly for the pain this decision caused to the hurt partner, family, and friends.

10. Encourage hurt partner to verbalize directly an acceptance of the apology from the unfaithful partner and to signify a beginning of the process of forgiveness even though hurt and anger are understandably felt.

11. Teach clients the "stop-and-share technique," in which the unfaithful partner stops all contact (including non-sexual contact) with lover. If this is impossible, he/she agrees to stop all personal discussions with lover. If contact does occur, unfaithful partner shares that fact with hurt partner before he/she asks. Elicit a verbal commitment from the unfaithful partner to implement this process.

affair-related intrusive thoughts. (23)

18. Hurt partner verify unfaithful partner's behavior to objectively test that partner's trustworthiness. Unfaithful partner will agree that such fact checking is a necessary part of reestablishing trust and will not attempt to dissuade hurt partner from checking up on him/her. (24)

19. Discuss context of the affair in session. (25, 26, 27)

20. Build a narrative of the affair by asking and answering questions about the initiation and course of the affair. (28, 29, 30, 31)

21. Attempt to learn from the affair by identifying in session the lessons that have been taught through this experience and planning how to use the lessons to improve the relationship. (32, 33, 34)

22. Devise and carry out personally meaningful rituals that aid relationship healing and symbolize moving forward together. (35, 36, 37)

—. _____
   _____
—. _____
   _____
—. _____
   _____

12. Assess current strengths and needs of relationship via interviews and/or questionnaires (e.g., Spanier Dyadic Adjustment Scale, Haynes Spouse Verbal Problem Checklist, LoPiccolo Sexual History Form, Snyder Marital Satisfaction Inventory, Olson PAIR, Straus Revised Conflict Tactics Scale).

13. Assess pre-affair functioning by asking each partner for relationship history. Questions could include: "How did the two of you meet?" "What attracted you to each other?" "What qualities or characteristics did you find that you liked about your partner?" "How did the two of you decide to get married?" "How was the adjustment after you got married?" "What have been the highs and lows during dating and your marriage prior to this affair?"

14. Increase caring behaviors and counter selective negative attention by assigning clients the "catch your partner pleasing you" exercise (i.e., client records at least one positive behavior each day by partner, and at least one by self).

15. Have each partner list exactly what changes each would like in order to feel more loved, respected, or

committed. Requests should be brief, and ask for observable increases in positive behavior rather than decreases in negative behavior.

16. Assign each client to list changes for self and other partner that would improve the relationship (e.g., using the "Areas of Change" questionnaire, Weiss & Birchler, 1975). Discuss the lists in conjoint sessions.

17. Assign each client to list an analysis of behaviors to be performed by self and partner that would benefit the relationship. Prioritize the list from *least* to *greatest* in terms of the effort, trust, and sacrifice each behavior would require (e.g., using Cost/Benefit Analysis, Birchler & Weiss, 1977). Seek mutual enactment of behaviors, requiring the *least* amount of trust and commitment first, following later with those of greater cost.

18. Teach clients the six components of time-out technique (i.e., *self-monitoring* for escalating feelings of anger and hurt, *signaling* to other partner that verbal engagement should end, *acknowledging* the need for other partner or self to disengage, *separating* to disengage, *cooling down* to regain control of emotions, *returning*

to controlled verbal engagement). Coach partners' practice in session, and assign for homework.

19. Discuss the need to plan what to do if lover attempts to contact them, and arrange for them to rehearse and role play in session likely reaction scenarios.

20. Assess current communication by having partners conduct a short, naturalistic conversation about the affair, with therapist observing but not interrupting. Teach communication skills, such as "I" statements and empathic listening, to foster constructive, nonaccusatory, nondefensive exchanges.

21. Assign hurt partner to list questions he/she has about the affair, to be presented in later sessions when the foundation has been laid for constructive exchanges.

22. Teach and model anxiety-management techniques to enable hurt partner to cope with intrusive thoughts (e.g., setting aside "worry" times; keeping a journal; using a thought-stopping exercise in which client says "Stop" to self and then substitutes a pleasant, relaxing thought for a disturbing one; using diaphragmatic breathing, where client focuses on slow breathing while concentrating on the diaphragm and

silently saying the word "calm" during exhalation)

23. Ask hurt partner to describe intrusive thoughts about the affair; have unfaithful partner listen empathically and support-ively (e.g., paraphrasing the content of hurt partner's statements, reflecting the emotional meaning of the hurt partners' statements, taking responsibility for causing distress).

24. Teach hurt partner to begin reestablishing trust by focusing on unfaithful part-ner's current behavior rather than own cata-strophic cognitions, acting as a detective if necessary (i.e., to reduce worrying through verifying).

25. Have partners discuss important life events that took place during the years immediately preceding the affair.

26. Ask each partner to describe his/her beliefs regarding monogamy, need for excitement, escapism, romantic love, admiration, and growth. Have partners discuss how these beliefs may have made an affair more likely.

27. Devise and enact treatment plan for addressing specific couple problems (such as relationship dissatisfaction or sexual dissatisfaction) by

reviewing pertinent sections of this *Treatment Planner*, negotiating plan with clients, and executing appropriate interventions.

28. Model hurt partner's questioning of unfaithful partner by making eye contact and asking questions in a calm, nonthreatening manner.

29. Contract with partners to establish an appropriate time frame for ending repeated questioning about the affair.

30. Teach hurt partner to ask factual questions (*who, what, where, when*) about the affair first, saving how and why questions for later. Appropriate questions might include: "What did the two of you do to become close?" "What were you anticipating?" "What did you think the limits to your behavior were?" "When did you decide to cross the limits?" "What were your vulnerabilities that made affair more likely?" "What was the typical pattern of how and where you'd meet?"

31. Teach partners "take-two" technique, in which discussion of details of affair is interrupted and repeated until the hurt partner can ask specific factual questions in a calm, nonthreatening manner, and unfaithful partner can answer questions directly

and succinctly, without
biaming hurt partner.

32. Have each partner describe
     what he/she learned about
     self that can be used to
     improve relationship.

33. Discuss learning histories
     that may have influenced
     susceptibility to affair. For
     example, "What did you
     learn about commitment
     and sensitivity to other's
     feelings from previous rela-
     tionships in your life?" "Are
     there any themes that run
     through these early rela-
     tionships?" "What did you
     learn about love from your
     parents?" "In what ways do
     these themes relate to your
     behavior around the affair?"

34. Ask each partner if there is
     a history of affairs in family
     of origin; if so, ask how this
     may have affected his/her
     feelings and behaviors
     about having (or learning
     about) the affair.

35. Using brainstorming tech-
     niques, help partners devise
     an appropriate ritual to sig-
     nify that unfaithful partner
     takes responsibility for the
     affair and asks for forgive-
     ness, and that forgiveness is
     granted by the hurt partner.
     This ritual should convey
     that the affair is forgiven
     but not forgotten and that
     both partners will now
     move forward.

36. Using brainstorming techniques, help partners devise an appropriate ritual to signify their mutual recommitment to an explicitly monogamous relationship.

37. Help partners devise plan for reclaiming places, people, or events tarnished by affair.

__. _____
_____

__. _____
_____

__. _____
_____

DIAGNOSIS SUGGESTIONS

Axis I: 309.24   Adjustment Disorder With Anxiety
309.0   Adjustment Disorder With Depressed Mood
309.28   Adjustment Disorder With Mixed Anxiety and Depressed Mood
296.xx   Bipolar I Disorder
301.13   Cyclothymic Disorder
302.71   Hypoactive Sexual Desire Disorder
296.xx   Major Depressive Disorder
V61.1   Partner Relational Problem
309.81   Posttraumatic Stress Disorder

_____   _____

Axis II: 301.7   Antisocial Personality Disorder
301.6   Dependent Personality Disorder
301.50   Histrionic Personality Disorder
301.81   Narcissistic Personality Disorder

_____   _____
_____   _____

INTOLERANCE

BEHAVIORAL DEFINITIONS

1. Rigid, consistent attitude on part of one or both partners that own behavior, beliefs, feelings, and attitudes are right and that other partner's behavior, beliefs, feelings, and opinions are wrong.
2. Frequent arguments, or disagreements that cause excessive tension.
3. Disagreements that are not restricted to specific problems but are interpreted as symbols of global problems (e.g., partner's personality, lack of love or respect).
4. Attempts to resolve problems that cause more tension and conflict than the original problems.
5. Efforts to coercively change partner's behavior that in turn produce coercive responses from the partner, thus causing the relationship to get stuck in a blaming cycle.
6. Expressions of affect that consist almost exclusively of protective emotions such as anger and vengeance, rather than empathy-enhancing emotions such as hurt and fear.

__. _____
   _____

__. _____
   _____

__. _____
   _____

A more expansive description of the interventions summarized in this chapter of the *Treatment Planner* can be found in Jacobson and Christensen (1997), Greenberg and Johnson (1988), Watzlawick, Weakland, and Fisch (1974), and Haley (1987).

LONG-TERM GOALS

1. Develop an attitude of acceptance toward each other, forgiveness toward shortcomings, and tolerance toward unique personality and behavior traits.
2. Allow for differences of opinion, beliefs and feelings without undue and ongoing conflict.
3. Recognize that each partner's problem behaviors are understandable ways of coping with the current relationship environment.
4. Express the underlying softer feelings that promote understanding rather than the more aggressive protective emotions that promote defensiveness and retaliation.
5. Accept the central differences in each other's approach to problems and the world.
6. Increase the meeting of some personal needs outside the relationship and decrease the exclusive reliance on the partner.

—. _____
_____

—. _____
_____

—. _____
_____

SHORT-TERM OBJECTIVES	THERAPEUTIC INTERVENTIONS
1. Express, verbally and in writing, overall level of relationship dissatisfaction and the specific areas of dissatisfaction. (1)	1. Assess current level of relationship satisfaction, using interview and/or self-report instruments (e.g., Relationship Satisfaction Questionnaire by Burns, Marital Adjustment Test by Locke and Wallace, or Dyadic Adjustment Scale by Spanier).
2. Identify the strengths and needs of the relationship. (2, 3)	2. Assess current strengths and needs of relationship via questionnaire. Options include Spouse Verbal Prob-
3. Describe the origination, development, and present state of the relationship. (4, 5)	

4. State degree of dissatisfaction with the marriage and own thoughts or actions taken toward breaking the relationship. (6)

5. Identify current problem areas and changes that self and other partner could make to improve the relationship. (7, 8)

6. Identify instances in which the definition of or reaction to a problem has become the main issue. Agree to refocus on the problem itself. (9)

7. Verbalize an understanding that each partner is reacting in understandable, but ultimately self-defeating, ways to the other's behavior. (10, 11)

8. Acknowledge that each partner has tried to force the other to change to meet the former's expectations. (12)

9. Verbalize agreement with partner practicing more acceptance of the other's unique feelings, beliefs, behavior, and opinions. (13, 14)

10. Avoid blame and "mind-reading" of partner by speaking only about own thoughts and feelings. (15)

11. Verbalize an understanding that soft emotions, such as hurt and vulnerability, precede hard/protective emotions, such as anger and resentment. (16, 17)

lem Checklist (Haynes et al., 1984), Sexual History Form (LoPiccolo, 1987), Marital Satisfaction Inventory (Snyder, 1979), PAIR (Olson, 1981), and Revised Conflict Tactics Scale (Straus et al., 1996).

3. Have partners identify the strengths of the relationship.

4. Assess the current developmental stage of relationship (e.g., early marriage, parents of young children, long-term marriage).

5. Assess the history of relationship. Appropriate questions might be: "How did the two of you meet?" "What attracted you to each other? "What qualities or characteristics did you find that you liked about your partner?" "How did the two of you decide to get married?" "What have been the highs and lows during dating and your marriage?"

6. Assess the steps each partner has taken toward divorce, using the Marital Status Inventory (Weiss and Cerreto, 1980) and by interviews with each partner about his/her sense of hope and vision of the future.

7. Have partners identify the current problem areas in the relationship.

12. Practice empathizing with partner by listening to and reflecting the soft emotion underlying the protective/hard emotion. (18)

13. Identify the ways in which central trait differences between self and partners create friction. (19, 20)

14. Verbally accept the inevitability of trait differences and discuss how to move toward acceptance of each other. (21)

15. Track and discuss successful adaptation to the central trait differences. (22)

16. Track and discuss unsuccessful adaptations to the behavioral trait differences. (23)

17. Demonstrate acceptance by describing the conflict as an external "thing," rather than blaming other partner. (24)

18. Demonstrate acceptance by describing positive aspects of other partner's problem behavior. (25, 26, 27)

19. Demonstrate acceptance of the problem pattern by admitting the inevitability of its reoccurrence, and by practicing the reoccurrence in session. (28, 29)

20. Increase understanding of the problem pattern by demonstrating it when not upset. (30, 31)

21. Practice problem enactment and discussion of soft

8. Assign each partner to list changes for self and the other that would improve the relationship (e.g., using Weiss and Birchler's 1975 Areas of Change questionnaire) and then review and discuss the lists in session.

9. Assist partners in identifying instances where their definition of or reaction to a problem became the main issue. Review and discuss these in session.

10. Provide partners with feedback on their strengths and weaknesses, highlighting those qualities of each that were either strengths or tolerated as weaknesses and which are now perceived as problems.

11. Teach that each partner's emotional and behavioral reactions are understandable, given their respective perceptions of the problem. "Bill believes that sex brings the two of you closer together, so if there is conflict, he thinks that sex might get things back on the right track. But Andrea, you reject Bill, believing that sex starts long before the bedroom and comes after conflict is resolved. So you both end up feeling hurt and angry."

12. Emphasize that the more each partner has tried to force the other to change, the worse their relationship

emotions following the "practiced" demonstration. (32, 33)

22. Identify acceptable resources outside the relationship for meeting some important personal needs. (34)

23. Practice alternative, constructive means for satisfying important personal needs within the relationship. (35, 36)

—. _____
_____

—. _____
_____

—. _____
_____

problems became. Discuss each partner's perspective on this idea.

13. Suggest to the partners that healing will only occur when they return to where all couples start relationships—by accepting and tolerating the other's strengths and weaknesses. Discuss each partner's perspective on this idea.

14. Present the equation "Pain + Accusation = Relationship Discord; Pain – Accusation = Acceptance" (Jacobson and Christensen, 1997). Have couple discuss the implications of the equation for their relationship.

15. Encourage each partner to express him/herself in terms of own thoughts and feelings, and to not presume to know or speak for the other's thoughts and feelings.

16. Discuss the difference between "hard" (i.e., protective) emotions such as anger, retribution, and resentment, and "soft" (i.e., vulnerable) emotions such as hurt, insecurity, and fear.

17. When client expresses a hard emotion, have him/her identify the soft emotion that underlies the hard emotion.

18. Have the listening partner paraphrase or reflect other

partner's disclosure of soft emotions.

19. Guide partners in discussing central trait differences between them, and the ways these differences have been causing problems (e.g., one partner is solution-oriented and one is expression-oriented).

20. Guide partners in discussing an event that will be occurring in the near future. Have them identify the ways behavioral and emotional problems resulting from their central trait differences will likely cause difficulty.

21. Encourage partners to accept the inevitability of their trait differences. Have them discuss what they can due to reduce the level of conflict, given that the trait differences are not going to go away.

22. When partners report that they handled a problem well at home, have them specifically elucidate what they thought or did differently that caused the situation to improve.

23. When partners report that a situation went poorly at home, have them specifically elucidate their respective thoughts, behaviors, and hard emotions that contributed to the difficulty.

24. Reframe the problematic interactional patterns as an external problem (an "it"), rather than as the fault of either partner.

25. Have one partner describe the positive features of the other's problematic behavior (i.e., the ways the other partner's behavior actually serves a positive function in the relationship).

26. If client has difficulty finding positive features, reframe the other partner's problematic behavior in terms of how it balances the client's behavior (e.g., a hyperresponsible man may get involved with a spontaneous woman).

27. Explain to clients that they each are bringing only one part of the balancing act to the relationship. Ask each whether there is anything that he/she can learn from the other partner's opposite, but balancing, behavior that formerly has been upsetting to client.

28. Explain to clients that no matter how they try to improve, they will sometimes fall back into their well-practiced, old patterns. Advise them to prepare for this and to not be too surprised or disappointed when the inevitable occurs.

29. Have couple practice falling back into their old patterns

in session. Ask each partner to express his/her thoughts and feelings, with the therapist emphasizing the naturalness of each person's perspective and response.

30. Assign each partner to enact or practice his/her problematic behaviors (e.g., Bill asking for sex following a tense time, even if he doesn't want sex) several times during the week, to get a sense of the pattern when he/she is not already upset.

31. Assign each partner to let the other in on the practiced problematic behaviors soon after the argument ensues, to prevent further escalation.

32. Have the partners take turns practicing problematic behaviors in session. Review and discuss the emotional reactions.

33. Review and discuss the emotional reaction to the practicing homework in the subsequent session.

34. Help clients identify acceptable ways of satisfying needs outside of the relationship, to reduce the pressure on the relationship to meet all of their core needs.

35. Help clients list ways in which they could satisfy needs arising from their soft emotions (e.g., relief from hurt or fear) within the relationship, without resort-

ing to destructive, hard
emotion–laced escalation.

36. Help clients rehearse, in
session, alternative means
of meeting needs arising
from their soft emotions.

__. _____
   _____

__. _____
   _____

__. _____
   _____

DIAGNOSIS SUGGESTIONS

Axis I

309.0	Adjustment Disorder With Depressed Mood
309.24	Adjustment Disorder With Anxiety
309.28	Adjustment Disorder With Mixed Anxiety and Depressed Mood
309.4	Adjustment Disorder With Mixed Disturbance of Emotions and Conduct
309.3	Adjustment Disorders With Disturbance of Conduct
305.00	Alcohol Abuse
303.90	Alcohol Dependence
300.4	Dysthymic Disorder
296.x	Major Depressive Disorder
V61.1	Partner Relational Problem
V61.1	Physical Abuse of Adult, 995.81 Victim
_____	_____

Axis II

301.7	Antisocial Personality Disorder
301.83	Borderline Personality Disorder
301.6	Dependent Personality Disorder
301.50	Histrionic Personality Disorder
301.4	Obsessive-Compulsive Personality Disorder
301.81	Narcissistic Personality Disorder
_____	_____
_____	_____

JEALOUSY

BEHAVIORAL DEFINITIONS

1. Concerns about loss of partner's affection, attention, and love to a rival.
2. Obsessive thoughts and/or frequent accusations about one's partner being with another person and being verbally and/or physically intimate with that person.
3. Monitoring of partner's activities (e.g., mileage, appointments, travel, money spent) based on suspicion of partner having an affair.
4. Controlling actions to restrict activity of partner (e.g., demanding partner stay at home; limiting the amount of money available to partner) based in fear of losing partner's attention.
5. Feelings of anger regarding a perceived loss of face to friends and family because partner did not show enough loyalty or attention to self.
6. Periodic angry outbursts directed at partner.
7. Blaming of partner for not being trustworthy or honest.
8. Depressive feelings regarding perceived loss of partner's attention, affection, and love.
9. Fear of being left alone and not being able to cope.
10. General anxiety and periodic physiological symptoms such as sleep disturbance, rapid heartbeat, tightness of chest, sweating, shortness of breath, dizziness, shakiness, and an empty feeling in the stomach.

If the level of jealousy is especially high, it may be advantageous for the therapist to see the jealous partner individually for at least a brief course of therapy before couple therapy is started. This may especially be the case with jealousy that immediately follows the discovery of an affair, or in cases of jealousy that have paranoid qualities.

___. _____
    _____
    _____
___. _____
    _____
    _____
___. _____
    _____
    _____

LONG-TERM GOALS

1. Eliminate or reduce the frequency of jealous thoughts and unfounded accusations of unfaithfulness.
2. Eliminate or reduce the frequency of controlling behaviors.
3. Eliminate or reduce the frequency of critical and angry comments associated with jealousy.
4. Eliminate or reduce the frequency of revengeful actions by the jealous partner (damaging property, destroying pictures of men/women who remind the jealous partner of the perceived rival).
5. Eliminate irrational blaming of partner.
6. Restore feelings of trust.

___. _____
    _____
    _____
___. _____
    _____
    _____
___. _____
    _____
    _____

SHORT-TERM OBJECTIVES

1. Verbalize a differentiation between the rational and irrational feelings of jealousy. (1, 2)
2. Clarify and identify the jealous and controlling behaviors in the relationship. (3, 4, 5)

THERAPEUTIC INTERVENTIONS

1. Ask the jealous partner to describe what seem to be his/her rational *and* irrational feelings of jealousy.
2. Ask the nonjealous partner to describe what seem to be the rational *and* irrational

3. Jealous partner list behaviors that can be changed by other partner to minimize jealousy. (6)

4. Discuss requests made by jealous partner and come to an agreement about the behavioral changes that seem reasonable to help minimize jealousy. (7, 8)

5. Clarify and identify the reasons for jealousy. (9, 10)

6. Jealous partner agree that jealousy is based in past hurts that are unrelated to current partner. (11)

7. Jealous partner identify hurts from partner that form a basis for current feelings of distrust and jealousy. (12)

8. Jealous partner begin a process of forgiveness for hurts from partner that have fostered distrust. (13)

9. Agree to focus on the relationship as it is now versus holding on to past hurts. (14)

10. Acknowledge that each partner must accept part of the responsibility for the future of the relationship (and for their satisfaction or dissatisfaction with it), independent of what happened in the past. (15, 16)

11. List changes that each partner could make to improve the relationship. (17, 18)

12. Reduce blame. (19)

feelings of jealousy of his/her partner.

3. Ask the nonjealous partner to describe jealous behaviors of his/her partner.

4. Ask the nonjealous partner to describe controlling behaviors of his/her partner.

5. Confirm that the jealous partner has engaged in the jealous and controlling behaviors described by the nonjealous partner.

6. Have jealous client list and prioritize what he/she would like other partner to do to minimize own feelings of jealousy.

7. Encourage jealous partner to reconsider some requests for change he/she has made regarding partner that may be irrational or overly demanding.

8. Encourage partners to jointly conclude which behaviors would be reasonable for reaching a goal of minimizing jealousy.

9. Explore the jealous partner's reasons for jealous feelings and allow the client to express anger to the therapist as often as necessary to believe that someone understands how he/she feels. (Developing such understanding can best take place in individual sessions prior to conjoint sessions, but such anger

13. Describe the basic rules of the relationship regarding each partner's interaction with others. (20)

14. Verbalize any changes that are necessary in the basic rules of interaction with others. (21, 22)

15. Nonjealous partner express understanding of jealous partner's reasonable feelings of threat to the relationship. (23)

16. Nonjealous partner alter behavior that is reasonably viewed by jealous partner as a potential threat to the relationship. (24)

17. Nonjealous partner increase frequency of positive, affirming comments to jealous partner as a means of building other's self-esteem. (25)

18. Nonjealous partner state a feeling of trust for jealous partner that counteracts other's jealous feelings and behaviors. (25, 26)

___. _____
_____

___. _____
_____

___. _____
_____

usually resurfaces repeatedly in conjoint sessions.)

10. Explore and resolve instances of hurt and abandonment in jealous partner's history that contribute to current feelings of distrust.

11. Help jealous partner separate feelings over past hurts from other people and the reaction of trying to protect self from hurt with current partner.

12. Assist jealous partner in identifying hurts from current partner that have fueled feelings of jealousy and distrust.

13. Encourage jealous client to begin a process of forgiveness for past hurts from partner and renew feelings of trust. Recommend reading *Forgive and Forget* (Smedes, 1991) and *How Good Do We Have To Be?* (Kushner, 1997).

14. Encourage both partners to focus on the here and now so as to minimize emphasis on past hurts and problems. Point out that though partners do not have to forget past wrongs, each should try to work toward the future.

15. Encourage each partner to accept some responsibility for satisfaction/dissatisfaction in the relationship.

16. Have each client describe ways that his/her actions may have led to the jealous partner's dissatisfaction.

17. Have each client describe things that he/she can do in the future that could make the relationship better.

18. Have nonjealous client engage in some behaviors that he/she feels would be appreciated by the partner, to provide clear examples of how he/she can take responsibility for helping the partner reduce jealousy.

19. Remind partners of the desirability of minimizing blame, especially blame expressed in a hostile way.

20. Have each partner describe the basic rules of how committed partners should behave when around other people and the degree of individual freedom each should have.

21. Educate partners on how the basic rules of the relationship may have to be altered if the life situation of one or both partners have changed markedly since the relationship began. (For example, life stage changes may affect the contacts that a partner may have with potential rivals. This problem can be especially acute for men whose wives have stayed at home for years raising children and then

enter college or the work-
place).

22. Help partners discuss the
    need for general agreement
    about the rule regarding
    emotional intimacy with
    others, as violations of it are
    often considered violations
    of trust.

23. Advise the nonjealous part-
    ner that though he/she may
    be the target of intermittent
    outbursts of anger by other
    partner, retaliation is unde-
    sirable, especially if there is
    some rational basis for the
    jealousy (e.g., nonjealous
    partner spends considerable
    time with an attractive per-
    son who could be considered
    a rival).

24. Confront nonjealous part-
    ner on being insensitive to
    jealous partner's insecurity
    by openly flaunting behav-
    iors that are threatening to
    the relationship.

25. Encourage nonjealous part-
    ner to provide reasonably
    frequent positive feedback
    to the other partner, espe-
    cially regarding issues that
    may lessen the partner's
    insecurity.

26. Educate partners that
    coping with problems of
    jealousy usually takes at
    least three to six months
    (and if there has been an
    affair, at least one year).
    Moreover, the nonjealous
    partner should be prepared

to cope with occasional setbacks.

___. _____
      _____
___. _____
      _____
___. _____
      _____

DIAGNOSTIC SUGGESTIONS

Axis I   309.0   Adjustment Disorder With Depressed Mood
              309.24   Adjustment Disorder With Anxiety
              309.28   Adjustment Disorder With Mixed Anxiety and
                         Depressed Mood
              309.4   Adjustment Disorder With Mixed Disturbance
                         of Emotions and Conduct
              309.3   Adjustment Disorders With Disturbance of
                         Conduct
              305.00   Alcohol Abuse
              303.90   Alcohol Dependence
              296.x   Bipolar I Disorder
              300.4   Dysthymic Disorder
              296.x   Major Depressive Disorder
              V61.1   Partner Relational Problem
              V61.1   Physical Abuse of Adult, 995.81 Victim

              _____   _____

Axis II   301.7   Antisocial Personality Disorder
              301.83   Borderline Personality Disorder
              301.81   Narcissistic Personality Disorder

              _____   _____
              _____   _____

JOB STRESS

BEHAVIORAL DEFINITIONS

1. Lack of respect for, and resultant lack of support of, supervisor.
2. Worry stemming from employer's threats to replace higher-salaried people with lower-salaried individuals through plant move or layoffs.
3. Frustration and helplessness stemming from competing company's product that could replace mainstay product of client's employer.
4. Anxiety caused by highly critical supervisor.
5. Anxiety stemming from employer's reduction of salaries due to decreasing profits.
6. Fears of being unable to master employer's new computer software system.
7. Concern and anger stemming from being moved to a less desirable office (e.g., one with less space, no windows).
8. Depression caused by being fired or laid off.
9. Inability to get along with peers at work.
10. Anxiety, frustration, and/or anger stemming from belief that own excellent and hard work is neither recognized nor rewarded.
11. Feelings of being discriminated against in terms of salary.
12. Intermittent depression, low energy, and sleep disturbance.
13. Lack of interest in sexual interactions.
14. Anger and intermittently explosive behavior.

__. _____
   _____
__. _____
   _____

—. _____

_____

LONG-TERM GOALS

1. Increase positive coping behaviors to reduce negative effects of work stress.
2. Increase positive attitudes about job and/or job alternatives.
3. Begin the process of searching for new and more desirable employment.
4. Obtain further training and/or retraining in work-related skills.
5. Reduce depressed mood and sleep disturbance while increasing energy level.
6. Reduce anger and terminate explosive outbursts at work and at home.

—. _____

_____

—. _____

_____

—. _____

_____

SHORT-TERM OBJECTIVES

1. Identify sources of irritability, depressed mood, and related depressive symptoms. (1, 2, 3, 4)

2. Identify sources of anger. (5, 6, 7, 8)

3. Explore whether some other individual problem (such as chronic depression, alcohol abuse, or sleep disorder) is the primary cause for unhappiness. (9)

THERAPEUTIC INTERVENTIONS

1. Assist client in listing all the work-related factors that make him/her depressed, angry, or discouraged.

2. Have client rank in order the employment factors that are most significant in causing his/her depression.

3. Develop a plan to address coping (e.g., increased recreational diversions, relaxation and deep-breathing

4. Use antidepressant or antianxiety medication as prescribed by physician. (10)

5. Consider a medical leave of absence from work responsibilities. (11, 12)

6. Assess and articulate own ability to handle technical requirements of job. (13, 14)

7. Enlist support of partner to help cope with job stress. (15, 16)

8. Contact agencies that provide instruction and training in areas relevant to current job. (17, 18)

9. Commit to further instruction and/or training to enhance job skills. (19)

10. Attend classes to obtain further education and vocational training. (20, 21)

11. Obtain information on computer-assisted home-teaching packages that would enhance job skills. (20, 21)

12. Make positive statements to self and others about the future. (22, 23, 24)

13. Decrease critical and complaining comments at work and at home. (25, 26, 27)

14. Make some acceptable change in work space to enhance physical and emotional aspects of working environment (e.g., put up new picture; clean office). (28, 29, 30)

techniques, physical exercise, assertiveness training, job transfer) with the most important work-related stressors.

4. Have partner rank in order the perceived causes (and associated factors) of depression in job-stressed client.

5. Have client list all of the job-related factors that make him/her angry.

6. Ask client to rank in order the most important job-related factors that make him/her angry.

7. Develop a plan to resolve (e.g., increased communication, assertiveness training, problem pinpointing/resolution training) causes for anger.

8. Have partner rank in order the perceived causes (and associated factors) of anger in the job-stressed client.

9. Explore with client and partner whether some other individual problem may be the primary cause for unhappiness.

10. Refer client to a physician for medication, and encourage him/her to take medication regularly.

11. Explore with client the advantages and disadvantages of taking medical leave.

12. Obtain input from client's partner about the advan-

___. _____

_____

___. _____

_____

___. _____

_____

tages and disadvantages of medical leave.

13. Ask client to obtain feedback about job performance from supervisor and peers, if doing so is practicable.

14. Have client assess his/her ability to perform the technical aspects of the job.

15. Have client advise partner how partner can best support him/her during next few months to assist in coping with job stress.

16. Explore whether partner can help situation by providing more financial support.

17. Refer client to agency that could provide assessment and/or job-skill training.

18. Refer client to educational institution with curriculum that could enhance job skills and/or enable client to obtain new degree or certificate.

19. Have client verbally commit to further training or education.

20. Support and reinforce client in efforts to pursue further training through an educational institution or via computer-assisted home instruction.

21. Explore with client possible alternative jobs that would be available upon completion of a course of study.

22. Assign client to make one positive statement to someone at work each day about the work and/or work environment.

23. Assign client to tell partner something positive about work each day.

24. Assign partner to support client's affirming of positive aspects of work and to add own positive perspective on client's work.

25. Advise client and partner to avoid making negative comments about work to colleagues.

26. Assign partner to provide support and reinforcement for client's decreasing negative comments about work.

27. Have client and partner list advantages of reducing complaining and critical comments about the work situation.

28. Explore with client possible acceptable ways of making his/her work space or office more pleasant and attractive.

29. Encourage client to take something attractive to work to decorate office (e.g. picture, poster, clock).

30. Encourage client to clean office and arrange things neatly.

___. _____

_____

—. _____

_____

—. _____

_____

DIAGNOSTIC SUGGESTIONS

Axis I: 309.24   Adjustment Disorder With Anxiety
309.0   Adjustment Disorder With Depressed Mood
309.28   Adjustment Disorder With Mixed Anxiety and
Depressed Mood
300.4   Dysthymic Disorder
300.02   Generalized Anxiety Disorder
296.x   Major Depressive Episode

_____   _____

_____   _____

Axis II: 301.82   Avoidant Personality Disorder
301.6   Dependent Personality Disorder

_____   _____

_____   _____

LIFE-CHANGING EVENTS

BEHAVIORAL DEFINITIONS

1. Individual distress (e.g., anxiety, depression) following an environmental event that requires adaptation.
2. Increased relationship distress due to perceived inability to support each other emotionally during the transition.
3. Increased relationship distress due to arguments resulting from the transition.
4. Relationship distress caused by change in employment situation (i.e., new responsibilities, increased travel, new employer, retirement, and/or changes in compensation).
5. Relationship distress caused by birth or adoption of a child and resultant significant change of lifestyle.
6. Relationship distress caused by a move to a new community and resultant severing of existing social support network and need for establishing a new one.
7. Relationship distress caused by a deterioration in health or debilitating injury and resultant significant changes in lifestyle distress.

—. _____
_____

—. _____
_____

—. _____
_____

LONG-TERM GOALS

1. Resolve negative feelings and relationship conflict generated by the life-changing event, making adaptive responses to the situation that foster individual and relationship growth.
2. Accept and adapt to the required transition.
3. Recognize the personal, relationship, and social benefits and drawbacks the life-changing event will produce.
4. Adapt to the life-changing event by using personal, relationship, and social resources.
5. Recognize the difference between transition problems that can be changed and those that cannot.
6. "Planfully" change or accept problems during the transition process.
7. Strengthen the relationship by being accepting of and supportive of each other.

—. _____

_____

—. _____

_____

—. _____

_____

SHORT-TERM OBJECTIVES	THERAPEUTIC INTERVENTIONS
1. Describe the life-changing event and its impact on each partner and the relationship. (1, 2)	1. Have each partner define the life-changing event and its meaning to him/her individually and to the relationship.
2. Verbalize acceptance of the fact that change is inevitable in everyone's life. (3)	2. Determine whether the event was expected or unexpected.
3. Define the stages of change in adaption to life-changing events (pre-contemplation, contemplation, action, and maintenance) and identify adaptation stage in reaction to current change stressor. (4)	3. Normalize the process of change in everyone's life by reviewing common changes that occur in the various developmental stages of life.

4. List ways of coping with the change that have been positive and productive. (5)

5. List ways of coping with the change that have been negative and counterproductive. (6)

6. Identify the positive and negative aspects of the life-change. (7)

7. Describe the anxiety and stress that the life-changing event has produced and explain how they have negatively affected the relationship. (8)

8. Identify the pros and cons of the life-changing event for self individually. (9, 10)

9. Identify the pros and cons of the life-changing event for the relationship. (11, 12)

10. Describe the day-to-day changes that the life-changing event will precipitate. (13)

11. Identify goals for short-term changes to be made in adapting to the current situation. (14)

12. Identify goals for long-term changes to be made in adapting to the current situation. (15)

13. Increase use of empathic listening skills in response to the other partner, stating what behaviors the partner could increase and those he/she could decrease in order to be supportive. (16, 17)

4. Administer Stages of Change questionnaire (University of Rhode Island Change Assessment, Prochaska et al., 1994) to determine which of the four stages of change best describes each partner's current adaptation to the transition (precontemplation, contemplation, action, or maintenance). Review and discuss the results with partners.

5. Ask each partner to describe his/her ways of coping with the current stressor that are productive.

6. Ask each partner to describe his/her ways of coping with the current stressor that are counterproductive.

7. Have partners discuss the positive and negative aspects of the life-changing event.

8. Teach that anxiety and strain are normal responses when coping with both good and bad life-changing events (e.g., the birth of a child, a job layoff).

9. Ask one partner to describe how the life-changing event may have positive effects for him/her individually, and have the other partner respond using supportive listener skills (i.e., paraphrasing, reflecting).

10. Ask one partner to describe

14. Identify support systems outside of the relationship that are currently available or can be added to assist in coping with the change. (18, 19)

15. Increase the use of individualized stress-reducing activities. (20, 21)

16. Increase the use of shared stress-reducing activities. (22)

17. Identify those problems that are within the couple's control, and those that must be accepted and adapted to. (23)

18. Pinpoint the changes that will be required in the personal, relational, and social domains. (24)

19. Using brainstorming techniques, develop at least two solutions to each change that is required. (25, 26)

20. Agree to a specific plan for enacting the selected solutions. (27)

21. Validate and empathize with other partner's feelings regarding the difficulty of accepting a problem that cannot be changed or controlled. (28, 29, 30)

22. Describe what in six months could be the best possible outcome to the life-changing event. (31)

23. Increase the frequency of mutually enjoyable activities with partner, to pro-

how the life-changing event may have negative effects for him/her individually, and have the other partner respond using supportive listener skills (i.e., paraphrasing, reflecting).

11. Ask each partner to describe how the life-changing event may have positive effects on the relationship.

12. Ask each partner to describe how the life-changing event may have negative effects on the relationship.

13. Help partners identify the concrete, day-to-day changes that the life-changing event will require.

14. Help each partner identify changes that will have to be made by self in the short term.

15. Help each partner identify changes that have to be made by self for the long term.

16. Have each partner describe what supportive behaviors he/she could increase during the transition, and have other partner respond using supportive listener skills.

17. Have each partner describe what negative behaviors he/she could decrease during the transition, and have other partner respond using supportive listener skills.

18. Explore the support sys-

mote relationship support
and harmony. (32)

—. _____
   _____

—. _____
   _____

—. _____
   _____

tems already in place outside of the relationship that
can aid both partners in
coping (e.g., friends, self-
help and support groups,
religious organizations).

19. Explore the support systems that can be added outside of the relationship to
aid both partners in coping
(e.g., friends, self-help and
support groups, religious
organizations).

20. Teach personal relaxation
techniques (e.g., diaphragmatic breathing, progres-
sive relaxation) that can be
used as coping mechanism,
to deal with the stress of
life-changing events.

21. Encourage each partner to
commit to regular individual stress-reducing activities (e.g., relaxation
techniques, exercise, music,
hobbies).

22. Encourage both partners to
commit to regular couple
stress-reducing activities
(e.g., foot rubs, social
engagements, walks, sex,
shared hobbies).

23. Help partners identify
which problems are within
their control and which
are not.

24. To set stage for solving
problems within partners'
control, have them pinpoint
adaptations required in the
personal, relational, and

social domains.

25. Teach partners to brain-storm at least two solutions for each problem before try-ing to solve the problem, and have them practice this in session.

26. Teach partners to evaluate the pros and cons of the brainstormed solutions, and have them practice this in session.

27. Teach partners to make a specific, pinpointed plan for solution, including a time in the future to evaluate the progress on the solution. Have them practice this in session.

28. For problems outside part-ners' control, role-play sup-port and acceptance by having one person "vent" about difficult aspects of coping with the transition and ask the listener to prac-tice validation skills (i.e., conveying that he/she understands and can empathize with the speaker's feelings, even if he/she does not agree).

29. When dealing with problems outside partners' control, instruct them to avoid trying to solve the external prob-lem, but instead support each other and problem-solve how they can accept the unchangeable problem.

30. If understanding or problem

solving is at an impasse,
have partners switch places
and then discuss the issue
from the other's perspective.

31. Ask partners to envision
themselves six months from
now and to describe their
functional adaptation to the
transition.

32. Assign partners to schedule
regular positive activities
with each other during the
transition period.

—. _____
   _____

—. _____
   _____

—. _____
   _____

DIAGNOSIS SUGGESTIONS

Axis I		
	309.24	Adjustment Disorder With Anxiety
	309.0	Adjustment Disorder With Depressed Mood
	309.28	Adjustment Disorder With Mixed Anxiety and Depressed Mood
	305.00	Alcohol Abuse
	303.90	Alcohol Dependence
	300.4	Dysthymic Disorder
	296.x	Major Depressive Disorder
	V61.1	Partner Relational Problem
	_____	_____
	_____	_____

LOSS OF LOVE/AFFECTION

BEHAVIORAL DEFINITIONS

1. Infrequent verbalizations of caring.
2. No verbalizations of love.
3. Overt questioning of own love for partner.
4. Absence of acts of kindness or thoughtfulness.
5. Little or no affectionate touching or kissing.
6. Infrequent sexual interaction.
7. Little time spent with partner on social or recreational activities.
8. Infrequent communication with partner regarding intimate matters.
9. Little planning for future events and activities with partner.
10. Avoidance of partner (e.g., often arrives home late at night, preferring work and coworkers over partner).

__. _____

_____

__. _____

_____

__. _____

_____

LONG-TERM GOALS

1. Overcome reasons for lack of caring and increase verbal, behavioral, and physical expressions of kindness, affection, and sexual intimacy.

2. Increase communication about all issues.
3. Increase acts of kindness and thoughtfulness between partners.
4. Increase time partners spend together in social and recreational activities.
5. Increase overall feelings and expressions of love and caring between partners.
6. Increase amount of physical intimacy between partners.
7. Increase amount of and satisfaction with sexual interaction.

___. _____
_____
_____
___. _____
_____
_____
___. _____
_____

SHORT-TERM OBJECTIVES

1. Identify reasons for lack of caring by partner. (1, 2, 3)
2. Begin to make restitution to partner for past wrongs. (4, 5, 6)
3. Agree to forgive other partner for hurts of the past. (7, 8, 9)
4. Read books on the process of forgiving another person. (10)
5. Commit to moving forward and to letting go of past issues. (11)
6. Increase eye contact with partner. (12, 13)
7. Decrease critical comments toward other partner. (14, 15, 16)

THERAPEUTIC INTERVENTIONS

1. Have each partner list the reasons that caring has eroded in the relationship.
2. Review with partners the reasons for the erosion of caring.
3. Address the possible need for individual therapy to help partners cope with any individual problems that interfere with the development of caring in the relationship.
4. Obtain commitment from both partners to make restitution for respective wrongs and transgressions in the relationship.
5. If one partner's actions have caused the other to experience jealousy, obtain a commitment from that

8. Increase positive verbal communication with other partner. (17, 18, 19)

9. Increase acts of kindness and helpfulness toward other partner (e.g., complete a task for partner, run an errand for partner). (20, 21, 22)

10. Increase expressions of praise, compliments, recognition, and gratitude to other partner. (23, 24)

11. Identify activities that self and partner would enjoy together. (25)

12. Engage in pleasurable social and recreational activities with partner. (26, 27)

13. Acknowledge that in unsatisfactory relationships changes in feelings generally follow changes in behavior. (28)

14. Verbalize realistic, attainable time goals for expression of feelings of affection, and intimacy. (29, 30)

15. Express commitment to not verbally coerce partner into sexual activities; acknowledge that sexual activities should be mutually agreed upon. (31, 32)

16. Verbalize an understanding that positive sexual interchanges generally follow when other aspects of the relationship improve, even without direct attention to the sexual relationship

partner to work especially hard at reassuring the other of his/her commitment to the relationship.

6. Have partners provide feedback to each other about specific actions that will help build mutual trust.

7. While acknowledging that some negative actions by partners are not easily forgotten, emphasize the positive role that forgiveness plays in intimate relationships.

8. Assist partners in forgiving and/or trying to forget past wrongs and hurts.

9. Educate partners regarding the negative effects of harboring anger and resentment over past wrongs and hurts.

10. Recommend that partners read the book *Forgive and Forget* (Smedes, 1991).

11. Obtain verbal commitment between partners and to the therapist to attempt to move forward and to put past issues behind them, at least for a specified period.

12. Teach partners to maintain eye contact with each other while speaking and listening.

13. Provide feedback to the partners about the extent to which each maintains eye contact with the other.

14. Educate partners regarding the very negative impact of

(unless there are specific sexual dysfunctions). (33)

17. Implement the techniques of sensate focus to increase the giving and receiving of physical pleasure. (34, 35, 36)

18. Read educational material regarding human sexuality and techniques of pleasuring. (35)

19. Increase the frequency of physical intimacy with partner, with the goal of pleasing him/her. (34, 35, 36)

—. _____
   _____
—. _____
   _____
—. _____
   _____

making critical and hostile comments to each other in therapy sessions or at home.

15. Obtain commitment from partners to minimize critical and hostile comments toward each other.

16. Advise partners that individual therapy may be needed as an adjunct or precursor to conjoint therapy, especially if expressions of anger by one or both partners in conjoint sessions cannot be contained.

17. Assist each partner in identifying the types of positive feedback that are pleasing to the other partner. (For example, some partners care about feedback about attire, while others regard such comments as irrelevant.)

18. Using behavior rehearsal techniques, have partners make positive comments about each other and about each other's positive behaviors.

19. Reinforce attempts by clients to be verbally supportive of each other.

20. Assist each partner in identifying the types of kind or helpful behaviors that are pleasing to the other partner. (For example, some partners care about getting the house cleaned, while

others do not care much about that.)

21. Obtain agreement from partners regarding specific helpful, thoughtful gestures each will perform during the week.

22. Reinforce attempts by partners to engage in nonverbal and nonphysical affectionate gestures.

23. Prompt mutual expressions of praise, compliments, recognition, and gratitude by partners during and between therapy sessions. Assign partners to log the giving and receiving of such comments, as a means of reinforcing the process.

24. Monitor partners' progress in mutually reinforcing each other and provide support for this effort.

25. Have partners describe social and recreational activities that they might like to do together.

26. Facilitate agreement between partners regarding a specific plan for some social or recreational activities together, even if they feel somewhat reluctant to do so initially.

27. Obtain feedback about how each partner felt during the mutual activity, and assist in helping expand such activities where possible.

28. Educate partners about the usual course of change,

emphasizing that initial changes in behaviors generally lead to subsequent changes in feelings and attitudes.

29. Educate partners regarding the need for patience when seeking changes in positive relationship feelings.

30. Assist partners in setting realistic goals about changes in caring and love.

31. Advise partners that forced sexual activities often backfire, with coercion by one partner frequently leading to resentment and withdrawal by the other.

32. Obtain commitment from both partners (and especially from the partner who has been the most frequent initiator of sexual activity) to only initiate and engage in sexual actions that are mutually agreed upon.

33. Explain to partners that sexual satisfaction in marital and long-term relationships often increases naturally when other aspects of the relationship, such as communication and nonsexual expressions of caring, improve.

34. If both partners are willing, teach them the techniques of sensate focus, where each partner alternates between giving and receiving sensual pleasure.

35. Assign partners to read,
either independently or
together, *Sexual Awareness*
(McCarthy and McCarthy,
1993) or *The Gift of Sex*
(Penner and Penner, 1981).

36. Monitor, review, and discuss
the partners' feelings sur-
rounding their increase in
physically intimate contact.

__. _____
     _____

__. _____
     _____

__. _____
     _____

DIAGNOSTIC SUGGESTIONS

Axis I	309.0	Adjustment Disorder With Depressed Mood
	309.24	Adjustment Disorders With Anxiety
	309.28	Adjustment Disorder With Mixed Anxiety and Depressed Mood
	296.x	Major Depressive Disorder
	V61.1	Partner Relational Problem
	V61.1	Physical Abuse of Adult, 995.81 Victim
	____	_____
	____	_____
Axis II	301.83	Borderline Personality Disorder
	____	_____
	____	_____

MIDLIFE CRISIS

BEHAVIORAL DEFINITIONS

1. Depressed mood and irritability.
2. Periodic crying spells.
3. Sleep disturbance.
4. Conflict between commitment to partner versus desire to be with another partner.
5. Conflict between staying in current job versus attempting to get another job.
6. Conflict over changing careers.
7. Conflict over goals (e.g., time spent with family members versus time on job versus time with friends).
8. Conflict over religious values and practices.
9. Concern about declining opportunity to have another sexual partner.
10. Concern about perceived decline in physical attractiveness.

—. _____
   _____
   _____
—. _____
   _____
   _____
—. _____
   _____

LONG-TERM GOALS

1. Reduce symptoms of depression and anxiety related to ambiguity of direction and values in life.

2. Resolve the conflict that precipitated the midlife crises.
3. Increase focus on living in accordance with specified goals and clarified values.
4. Recognize advantages that usually come only with maturity.
5. Reach beyond self and become connected or reconnected to partner, family members, and/or religious community.
6. Rediscover an appreciation for and commitment to the existing intimate relationship.

—. _____
_____
_____

—. _____
_____
_____

—. _____
_____

SHORT-TERM OBJECTIVES

1. Verbalize the thoughts that produce anxiety and worry over the future. (1, 2)
2. Implement the use of positive, reality-based cognitive messages to replace distortions that precipitate anxiety regarding the future. (3)
3. Articulate what values are most important in own life and what forms the basis for those values. (4)
4. State how current and past life has been in harmony with prioritized values. (5)
5. State how current and past life has been in disharmony with stated values. (6)
6. List changes that need to be made in work, relationships, family, recreation, and spiri-

THERAPEUTIC INTERVENTIONS

1. Probe for cognitive distortions that lead to anxiety and uneasiness.
2. Assign client to keep daily diary of thoughts that precipitate anxious and depressed feelings.
3. Assist client in developing a list of positive cognitive messages that are reality-based, and reinforce client's feelings of confidence about self and the future.
4. Assist partners in identifying what values are most important to them and whether a foundational basis exists for those values.
5. Review client's current and past life to determine

tuality to bring life into harmony with values. (7)

7. Verbalize spiritual beliefs and the degree of harmony felt with and strength gained from those beliefs. (8)

8. Talk with partner about spiritual beliefs and make a plan to achieve greater closeness with a higher power and a community of believers. (9)

9. Identify developmental history of goals held for self and perceived expectations of others for self. (10, 11, 12)

10. Other partner describe goals he/she has had for client. (13)

11. Describe goals that have remained unfulfilled and the feelings associated with that lack of fulfillment. (14)

12. Verbalize acceptance that some goals cannot be attained. (15)

13. List realistic alternative goals for future attainment and steps needed to reach them. (16, 17, 18)

14. Clarify and articulate why future goals are of value to self, partner, and relationship. (18, 19, 20)

15. Identify the advantages that come with maturity. (21, 22)

16. Verbalize acceptance of own aging and sense of peace over it. (21, 22, 23)

17. Identify acts of kindness

degree of congruity between his/her values and lifestyle.

6. Review client's current and past life to determine how life decisions have been in conflict with stated values.

7. Assist partners in identifying how various areas of life could be changed to achieve greater harmony with values.

8. Explore each partner's spiritual life and the degree of satisfaction he/she feels with it.

9. Encourage partners to discuss their spiritual beliefs with each other, and to formulate a plan for increasing their closeness to a higher power and a community of believers.

10. Have client describe his/her goals and wishes as a late teen and young adult, and how these may have changed over the years.

11. Have client describe the goals and wishes his/her parents had for client.

12. Have client describe perceived goals that partner had for him/her.

13. Obtain feedback from client's partner regarding goals and wishes he/she has for client.

14. Have client describe his/her unfulfilled goals.

15. Assist client in identifying goals that probably are not

that could be done for others, and articulate benefits of self-sacrifice and focusing on others. (24, 25)

18. Spend some time each week doing something for someone else, even if the act of kindness is a small one. (26)

19. Clarify and articulate the beneficial value of giving more time to family relationships. (27)

20. Increase contact with immediate and/or extended family members. (28)

21. Report a sense of value and satisfaction with giving of self to family members. (29)

22. Verbalize an understanding of the value of touching in intimate human relationships. (30)

23. Increase level of physical affection with intimates. (31, 32)

24. Verbalize the value of—and own renewed commitment to—relationship with partner. (33)

25. Articulate feelings and thoughts associated with current employment, and vision for the future in this work. (34)

26. List possible alternative employment directions for the future, and advantages and disadvantages of each. (35)

27. Verbalize a commitment to accept current employment

realistically attainable and that must be accepted as such. Review and discuss client's feelings associated with this reality.

16. Have client list goals that are still realistically attainable and plans he/she has to reach them.

17. Assist client in assigning values to alternative goals.

18. Assign client to consult other individuals whom he/she respects regarding possible alternative goals for self and their value.

19. Assist client in determining the likelihood of attaining alternative goals.

20. Obtain feedback from each partner about the perceived value of alternative goals to self and relationship.

21. Have client describe attributes of an older individual whom he/she respects.

22. Help client identify advantages that usually come with maturity (e.g., less impulsive judgments, greater experiential wisdom, broader views of values in life, knowledge of more lifestyle alternatives, more concern about others).

23. Explore and resolve client's possible feelings of anxiety and fatalistic depression related to aging, including fear of physical deterioration and/or declining health.

situation without resentment or negative self-talk regarding lack of accomplishment or future advancement. (36)

28. State a concrete plan for exploring other career opportunities that have been identified as challenging and appropriate. (37)

—. _____

_____

—. _____

_____

—. _____

_____

24. Assist client in identifying things that he/she might do for others, thereby reducing focus on self.

25. Educate client regarding the value to self of acts done for the benefit of others.

26. Assign client to do something for others each week.

27. Assist client in identifying the benefits of increased contact with immediate and extended family members.

28. Encourage client to write, call, or visit immediate or extended family members.

29. Educate client regarding the positive impact of increased contact with family members.

30. Teach client the value of touching in intimate relationships (i.e., increases partners' feelings of importance; enhances mutual feelings of closeness, warmth, caring, and security).

31. Encourage client to commit self to being more physically affectionate to intimates.

32. Assign client to engage in some act of physical affection at least every few days.

33. Assist client in rediscovering the positive aspects of maintaining current intimate relationship between self and partner.

34. Explore partners' feelings associated with client's cur-

rent employment and what impact it has on each partner and the family.

35. Assist client in identifying possible alternative career directions and the advantages and disadvantages of each possibility for self and relationship.

36. Help client accept and commit to present employment with a sense of satisfaction.

37. Assist client in developing a plan for responsibly exploring alternative career directions while avoiding impulsive actions that could have devastating long-term consequences.

—. _____
_____

—. _____
_____

—. _____
_____

DIAGNOSTIC SUGGESTIONS

Axis I:	309.0	Adjustment Disorder With Depressed Mood
	309.24	Adjustment Disorders With Anxiety
	309.28	Adjustment Disorder With Mixed Anxiety and Depressed Mood
	300.4	Dysthymic Disorder
	300.02	Generalized Anxiety Disorder
	296.x	Major Depressive Disorder
	V61.1	Partner Relational Problem
	_____	_____
	_____	_____

ONE PARTNER UNWILLING TO ATTEND THERAPY

BEHAVIORAL DEFINITIONS

1. Individual distress over the relationship as evidenced by emotional (e.g., anger, tension), cognitive (e.g., blaming), and behavioral (e.g., arguing, withdrawal) difficulties.
2. Refusal by other partner to attend counseling sessions.
3. Inability of other partner to attend counseling sessions, due to work schedule conflict.

—. _____
   _____
—. _____
   _____
—. _____
   _____

LONG-TERM GOALS

1. Improve acceptance of and satisfaction with the relationship, changing those things that are under one's control.
2. Enact relationship-enhancing behaviors at home.
3. Increase rewarding activities with and without partner.
4. Learn to organize thoughts and behaviors in specific situations to accomplish desired outcomes.
5. Change thinking and behavioral patterns that create conflict or interfere with attempts to achieve desired outcomes.

6. Adapt to central differences between each other by accepting and working around them.
7. Identify the softer emotions (e.g., hurt and vulnerability) that promote the overt, protective emotions (e.g., anger and resentment).
8. Increase resourcefulness by identifying means of meeting personal needs outside the relationship.
9. Increase resourcefulness by identifying means of meeting personal needs through means other than "hard" emotion expression.

—. _____
   _____
—. _____
   _____
—. _____
   _____

SHORT-TERM OBJECTIVES

1. Invite partner to participate in treatment sessions. (1, 2, 4)
2. Verbalize any fears about informing partner of treatment or having him/her attend sessions. (3)
3. Give permission for therapist to invite partner to attend counseling sessions to provide information that might be useful to the presenting client's treatment. (5)
4. Describe the origination, development, and present state of the relationship. (6, 7)
5. Express verbally and in writing the overall level of relationship dissatisfaction

THERAPEUTIC INTERVENTIONS

1. Determine whether the client has asked his/her partner to attend therapy.
2. Have client detail the context under which he/she asked the partner to attend counseling sessions (when, where, what context).
3. Assess potential dangers (such as fear of assault) of client attempting to engage partner in therapy.
4. If appropriate, use role-playing techniques to help client appropriately ask partner to attend counseling sessions. For example: "I care about you, and I'm concerned that our relationship is at risk. I'm going to attend therapy to work on improving our relationship, and I'd

and the specific areas of dissatisfaction. (8)

6. Describe any suspicions regarding the partner having had an affair. (9)

7. Verbalize any incidents of physical, sexual, or emotional abuse or intimidation by other partner. (10)

8. Report any steps taken to dissolve the relationship. (11)

9. Identify the pros and cons of remaining in the relationship versus separation or divorce. (12)

10. Identify current problem areas in the relationship. (13)

11. Specify the problem areas that are under one's control. (14, 15)

12. Identify and list behavioral changes for self that would enhance the relationship. (16, 17)

13. Plan for performing relationship-beneficial behaviors, starting with those that are least costly to enact. (18)

14. Generate lists of preferred recreational activities that could be done alone, with partner, or with others. (19)

15. Discuss with partner the desire to increase rewarding activities. (20, 21)

16. Increase the number of rewarding activities that do not require participation by the partner. (22)

appreciate your being willing to come with me."

5. If client gives permission, call partner and invite him/her to attend sessions to provide information that might be useful to the presenting client's treatment.

6. Assess the developmental stage of the couple's relationship (e.g., early marriage, parents of young children, long-term marriage).

7. Assess client's history of satisfaction with the relationship (e.g., recent changes, including those in relationship; happiness and thoughts about divorce; expectations of marriage and divorce).

8. Assess client's current relationship satisfaction, using interview and/or self-report instruments (e.g., Relationship Satisfaction Questionnaire by Burns, Marital Adjustment Test by Locke and Wallace, 1959, or Dyadic Adjustment Scale by Spanier, 1976).

9. Assess relationship for the presence or suspicion of affairs (see Infidelity and Jealousy chapters of this *Planner*).

10. Assess relationship for incidents of violence or intimidation (see Psychological, Physical, or Sexual Abuse chapters of this *Planner*), through clinical interview

17. Verbalize an understanding of the rationale for situational analysis. (23)

18. Complete situational analysis homework to increase efficacy at effecting positive outcomes in situations at home. (24, 25)

19. Identify whether self's thoughts or conclusions promote problem resolution, are directly relevant to the situation, and are based on reality. (26)

20. Verbalize self-talk conclusions that promote problem resolution, are directly relevant to the situation, and are based on reality. (27)

21. Choose desired outcomes that are realistic and achievable. (28)

22. Verbally generate a generalizable lesson to be learned from the specific situational analysis and apply it to other situations of conflict. (29, 30)

23. Recognize that soft emotions, such as hurt and vulnerability, precede hard or protective emotions, such as anger and resentment. (31, 32)

24. Demonstrate acceptance by treating the problem as an external "thing," rather than blaming partner. (33)

25. Demonstrate acceptance by listing positive aspects of partner's problem-causing behavior. (34, 35, 36)

and/or use of an inventory (e.g., Revised Conflict Tactics Scale by Straus, et al.).

11. Assess the steps each partner has taken toward divorce by interviewing client about his/her sense of hope and vision of the future and/or by using a questionnaire (e.g., Marital Status Inventory by Weiss and Cerreto, 1980).

12. Have client state his/her point of view on (a) the pros and cons of preserving the relationship, and (b) the pros and cons of separation or divorce.

13. Assist client in identifying the current problem areas in the relationship.

14. Educate client that all individual therapy can be a form of relationship therapy, because changes on the part of one partner cause changes in the nature of the relationship.

15. Assist client in identifying which current problems he/she has at least some influence over (e.g., communication problems, anger problems).

16. Have client list general changes that he/she could make to improve the relationship (e.g., complete the "It would please my partner if I . . ." section of Weiss and Birchler's 1975 Areas of Change Questionnaire). Review and discuss the list

26. Identify resources outside the relationship that can meet important personal needs. (37)

27. Discuss and practice alternative means (i.e., those not involving problem-causing pattern) of satisfying important personal needs within the relationship. (38, 39)

—. _____
   _____

—. _____
   _____

—. _____
   _____

with the client.

17. Have client rate the behaviors that he/she could perform to benefit the relationship, including estimates of the perceived sacrifice entailed in performing each of them (as in Weiss' 1975 Cost/Benefit Analysis).

18. Arrange list of beneficial behaviors from least to greatest in terms of the amount of sacrifice that enactment would require. Assign client to perform three to five of these behaviors per week.

19. Assign client to generate a list of desired activities in the following categories: (a) to be done alone; (b) to be done with partner; (c) to be done with partner and other family members; (d) to be done with partner and nonfamily members; and (e) to be done with nonfamily members (e.g., by completing the Inventory of Rewarding Activities by Weiss).

20. Using role-playing techniques, help client rehearse asking partner to engage in positive activities together.

21. Assign client to ask partner to engage in positive activities together, and to report his/her response at the next session.

22. Assign client to increase the number of positive activities he/she does alone or

with nonfamily members.

23. Describe for client the goal of situational analysis in the following manner: "Although we try to get large payoffs, like having a happy marriage, these payoffs are achieved one small situation at a time. To work toward the big goals, try to make changes in the way you think and behave in small, observable situations that have a beginning, middle, and end." Have client repeat rationale in his/her own words.

24. Assign client situational analysis homework that asks him/her to identify (*a*) a problematic situation (e.g., a description of the beginning, middle, and end of an observable situation); (*b*) three cognitions that occurred during the situation; (*c*) the client's behavior during the situation; (*d*) the actual outcome; and (*e*) the desired outcome.

25. Ask client to read aloud from the situational analysis homework sheet, and paraphrase his/her statements to make sure that the therapist understands the key elements of the situational analysis.

26. Have client state whether each thought was (*a*) helpful in getting the desired outcome; (*b*) anchored to the specific situation described (i.e., is situationally-specific,

not global); and (c) accurate (i.e., overt evidence can be marshaled to support it).

27. If any thoughts do not meet all three criteria, help client rework the thought so that it does meet all three criteria. For example, "She's always on my back," can become "There's something happening here that she thinks is important."

28. Have client state whether the desired outcome was achievable (i.e., under his/her control). If not, help client rework the desired outcome so that it is achievable. For example, "I want him to listen to me when I'm upset," can become "I want to ask him to schedule a time for us to talk about problems that we're having."

29. Ask client to summarize the situation by deriving a lesson to be learned from the situational analysis.

30. Help client apply the lesson to other situations.

31. Discuss with client the difference between "hard" (i.e., protective) emotions, such as anger, retribution, and resentment, and "soft" (i.e., vulnerable) emotions, such as hurt, insecurity, and fear.

32. When client expresses a hard emotion, have him/her identify the soft emotions that underlie the hard emotion.

33. Reframe for client the prob-

<

lematic interactional patterns as an external problem (an "it"), rather than as the fault of either partner.

34. Ask client to describe the positive features of the partner's problematic behavior (i.e., the ways the partner's behavior actually serves a positive function in the relationship).

35. If client has difficulty finding positive features, reframe the partner's problematic behavior in terms of how it balances the client's behavior (e.g., a hyperresponsible man may get involved with a spontaneous woman).

36. Explain to client that each partner brings only one part of the balancing act to the relationship, and ask if anything can be learned from the partner's opposite, but balancing, behavior that formerly has been upsetting to client.

37. Ask client to list ways of satisfying own needs outside of the relationship, to take pressure off the relationship to meet all his/her core needs.

38. Help client list ways that he/she could get needs arising from soft emotions (e.g., protection, relief from hurt) met within the relationship without resorting to destructive, hard emotion-laced

escalation.

39. Have client role-play alter-
    native means of satisfying
    needs arising from his/her
    soft emotions.

___. _____

_____

___. _____

_____

___. _____

_____

DIAGNOSIS SUGGESTIONS

Axis I	309.0	Adjustment Disorder With Depressed Mood
	309.24	Adjustment Disorder With Anxiety
	309.28	Adjustment Disorder With Mixed Anxiety and Depressed Mood
	309.3	Adjustment Disorders With Disturbance of Conduct
	305.00	Alcohol Abuse
	303.90	Alcohol Dependence
	296.x	Bipolar I Disorder
	300.4	Dysthymic Disorder
	296.x	Major Depressive Disorder
	V61.1	Physical Abuse of Adult, 995.81 Adult
	V61.1	Partner Relational Problem
	309.81	Posttraumatic Stress Disorder
	_____	_____
	_____	_____
Axis II	301.7	Antisocial Personality Disorder
	301.83	Borderline Personality Disorder
	301.6	Dependent Personality Disorder
	301.81	Narcissistic Personality Disorder
	_____	_____
	_____	_____

PARENTING CONFLICTS—ADOLESCENTS

BEHAVIORAL DEFINITIONS

1. Frequent arguments between partners about parenting, or disagreements that interfere with effective parenting of adolescent.
2. Lack of agreement between parents regarding strategies for dealing with various types of negative adolescent behaviors.
3. Ineffective parental responses to negative adolescent behavior (i.e., efforts that do not result in the desired outcomes).
4. Inability of partners to discuss and support each other's parenting efforts.

___. _____
   _____
___. _____
   _____
___. _____
   _____

LONG-TERM GOALS

1. Discuss and agree on the implementation of joint parenting strategies.
2. Create a positive, supportive parent-adolescent home environment.

A more expansive description of the interventions summarized in this chapter can be found in the work of Patterson and Forgatch (1987), Forgatch and Patterson (1987), and Robin and Foster (1989).

3. Consistently reinforce positive adolescent behavior and punish negative behavior.
4. Share ideas about parenting strategies and support each other's parenting behavior.
5. Make and enforce consistent house rules.

—. _____

   _____

—. _____

   _____

—. _____

   _____

SHORT-TERM OBJECTIVES

1. Specify adolescent behavior problems. (1, 2, 3)
2. Verbalize parenting philosophy and expectations for adolescent. (4)
3. Identify parent-adolescent behavior patterns that may be contributing to the negative behavior. (5)
4. Identify family, school, or parenting factors that may be contributing to the negative behavior. (6, 7)
5. Discuss how relationship functioning affects and is affected by parenting difficulties. (8, 9)
6. Identify the strengths and weaknesses of partners working together as a team. (10, 11)
7. Improve parenting knowledge by reading assigned

THERAPEUTIC INTERVENTIONS

1. Ask parents to describe their main concerns about the adolescent's problem behavior, and its history. Therapist's questions might include: "When did problem behavior start?" and "How has it changed across time?"
2. Ask parents to specifically detail the extent of the adolescent's problem behavior. Therapist's questions might include: "How frequently and intensely does problem behavior occur?" "How long does it last?" "In which situations does it occur?"
3. Identify specific areas of conflict and problem behaviors by having parents complete questionnaire assessments such as Issues Checklist (Robin and Foster, 1989) or Conflict Behavior Question-

books on parenting adolescents. (12, 13)

8. Monitor adolescent's whereabouts, and identify any deficiencies in monitoring. (13, 14, 15)

9. Identify an adolescent behavior that partners would like to reinforce, and track its occurrence as well as antecedents and consequences. (16)

10. Increase the frequency of contingently reinforcing positive adolescent behavior. (17)

11. Increase the frequency of positive social or activity-oriented interactions with adolescent. (18, 19)

12. Identify a behavior in adolescent that partners would like to discourage, and track its occurrence as well as antecedents and consequences. (20)

13. Establish and implement consequences (punishments) for negative adolescent behavior. (21)

14. List some natural and logical negative consequences (punishments) that could apply to a specific misbehavior. (22)

15. Each parent identify, examine, and then pledge to terminate any negative behavior that he/she is modeling and that the adolescent is imitating. (23)

naire (Prinz, Foster, Kent, and O'Leary, 1979).

4. Identify (*a*) each partner's parenting philosophy and strategy, and (*b*) each partner's expectations for adolescent's behavior (e.g., "Adolescents should never be disrespectful toward their parents") via interviews and questionnaires such as Family Beliefs Inventory (Roehing and Robin, 1986) or Parent-Adolescent Relationship Questionnaire (Robin, Koepke, and Moye, 1990).

5. Identify parent-adolescent behavioral patterns that may be maintaining the problem (e.g., unintentionally reinforcing problem behavior through nagging or emotional parenting).

6. Identify social context factors that may be maintaining the problem (e.g., family transitions, inconsistent rules, school or social difficulties).

7. Identify parents' stressors that may be maintaining the problem (e.g., unemployment, substance use, depression).

8. Have parents indicate ways their relationship conflict has a negative impact on their adolescent's behavior.

9. Have parents describe how their adolescent's behavior

16. Check with partner regularly concerning parenting and keep a log of these interactions. (24, 25, 26)

17. Use argument-control strategies to increase the productivity of parenting conversations. (27)

18. Report instances of constructive and supportive conversations with partner regarding current parenting experiences. (28, 29)

19. Agree with partner to support each other's parenting. (30, 31, 32)

20. Agree with partner to discuss parenting disagreements only when discussion is likely to be constructive. (33)

21. Regularly discuss and problem-solve parenting strategies for handling misbehavior. (34)

22. Reach agreement with partner regarding the exact nature of a parenting problem before trying to resolve it. (35)

23. Demonstrate empathy and respect for other partner's point of view by paraphrasing or reflecting his/her position before responding. (36)

24. Agree with partner to discuss only one parenting problem at a time, and only after it has been pinpointed. (37)

25. Brainstorm with partner several possible parental

problems impact on their relationship conflict.

10. Using behavioral rehearsal techniques, have the partners attempt to solve a major parenting problem. Quietly observe and note skills and deficiencies.

11. Review and discuss the problem-solving interaction. Have partners note their strengths and weaknesses as a parenting team.

12. Assign parents to read *Parents and Adolescents: Living Together. Vol I: The Basics* and *Vol II: Family Problem Solving* (Patterson and Forgatch, 1987).

13. Assign parents to coordinate monitoring of their adolescent's activities, keeping track of where he/she is, who he/she is with, what they are doing, and when they will be home.

14. Assign parents to record their joint monitoring efforts.

15. Have parents discuss their successes at monitoring and to identify times and situations where the monitoring needs to be improved.

16. Have parents identify one of their adolescent's behavior patterns that they would like to reinforce. Assign them to record its occurrence every day for a week, and to note the behaviors or situations that precede it

interventions for the misbehavior. (38)

26. Evaluate with partner various possible solutions to the adolescent's problematic behavior, and then choose one solution. (39)

27. Agree with partner to enact solution, and then evaluate its effectiveness. (40, 41)

28. Use problem-solving skills (i.e., problem definition, brainstorming, evaluation of alternatives, solution enactment, and enactment evaluation) in discussions with adolescent. (42)

29. Identify and challenge unreasonable beliefs and expectations about adolescent behavior. (43, 44)

30. Conduct regular family problem-solving meetings. (45, 46)

31. In company with partner, establish consistent house rules. (47)

32. In company with partner, establish a regular dinnertime and foster the expectation that all family members will take part. (48, 49)

—. _____
_____

—. _____
_____

—. _____
_____

(i.e., antecedents) and follow it (i.e., consequences).

17. Help parents decide on an appropriate reward (e.g., praise, use of the car, increase in allowance) to reinforce the positive behavior. Have parents rehearse praising positive behavior pattern in session, and provide them with feedback.

18. Assign parents to increase amount of focused, adolescent-centered recreational activity with the adolescent experiencing difficulty.

19. Assign each parent to increase the number of parent-initiated, casual, positive conversations with the adolescent experiencing difficulty.

20. Ask parents to identify one of their adolescent's problem behaviors that they would like to decrease. Assign them to record its occurrence every day for a week, and to note the behaviors or situations that precede it (i.e., antecedents) and follow it (i.e., consequences).

21. Have parents decide on an appropriate negative consequence (e.g., loss of privilege, five-minute work chore) to contingently discourage negative behavior.

22. Teach parents to establish logical and natural consequences to adolescent misbehavior (e.g., break curfew

→ lose privilege to go out;
make a mess → clean up
the mess).

23. If parents are modeling for
the adolescent the behavior
they would like to extin-
guish (e.g., yelling, being
sarcastic), have them contract to change their own
behavior before trying to
change the same behavior
in the adolescent.

24. Assign parents to confer
with each other at least
once a day regarding the
adolescent's behavior.

25. Encourage parents to plan a
mutually acceptable time to
confer, to avoid casual conversations at times when
arguments are likely to
erupt (e.g., immediately
upon arriving home in the
evening).

26. Instruct partners to track
their satisfaction with the
daily check-ins and bring in
the tracking sheet to treatment sessions.

27. Using modeling and behavior rehearsal, assist partners
in practicing argument control (e.g., calling time-out,
using "I" messages in place
of "you" messages). Assign
partners to employ tech-
nique to cool off during parenting discussions if either
believes that conversation is
becoming unsupportive.

28. Have partners role-play discussions they will have
when the adolescent is well

behaved. Have the supportive partner ask the other what the adolescent has been doing and then support his/her parenting behaviors.

29. Have partners role-play discussions they will have when the adolescent displays negative behavior. Have the supportive partner ask, in a supportive, non-threatening manner, about the specifics of the misbehavior.

30. During role-playing exercises for dealing with adolescent misbehavior, have the supportive partner ask, in a supportive, non-threatening manner, how the other partner dealt with the misbehavior and whether the supportive partner can do anything in the future to help.

31. Have partners contract to support each other's parenting by not interfering during the other's parent-adolescent interactions, and by not interfering with the other's decisions (i.e., avoiding splitting of parents' unity).

32. Help partners identify what each can do to help the other in challenging situations (e.g., when adolescent is disrespectful).

33. Have partners contract to put disagreements over parenting strategy on hold until

the situation has ended and
they can meet privately, and
both partners are calm and
able to problem-solve without accusations or defen-
siveness.

34. Assign partners to schedule
    parenting problem-solving
    discussions for two or three
    times per week.

35. Have partners role-play
    using pinpointing skills
    (i.e., statements that are
    specific, observable, and ask
    for increases in behavior) to
    specifically identify the pre-
    senting problem.

36. Have partners role-play the
    speaker-listener technique,
    where the listener does not
    respond with own thoughts
    until he/she has para-
    phrased the speaker's posi-
    tion to that person's
    satisfaction.

37. Advise partners to limit
    themselves to solving one
    problem at a time.

38. Encourage each partner
    to brainstorm at least two
    possible solutions to each of
    the adolescent's problem
    behaviors.

39. Have partners role-play
    choosing a solution together
    by judging the advantages
    and disadvantages of each
    possible solution.

40. Help partners plan together
    on how to enact solutions.

41. Have partners establish a
    time to review the progress

of the solution, and to troubleshoot the solution as necessary.

42. Arrange for the adolescent to attend family sessions as necessary. Have parents employ communication skills in problem-solving with the adolescent as well as each other (i.e., defining problem, brainstorming, evaluating of alternatives, enacting solution, and evaluating solution).

43. Assign parents to track their thoughts and emotional reactions during problematic situations with their adolescent.

44. Identify and challenge unreasonable assumptions by (*a*) asking parents to provide evidence for their truth and (*b*) persuasively illuminating the illogical premise involved. For example, "If my daughter stays out late, she will become pregnant or a drug addict," can be replaced by "I can make my opinions and the house rules known, but ultimately her behavior is up to her."

45. Assign parents to initiate regular family meetings for constructive problem-solving and evaluation of earlier contracts. Family meetings should be time-limited (starting with 15 minutes) and should observe set ground rules. See page 117 of *Parents and*

Adolescents: Living Together. Vol II: Family Problem Solving (Patterson and Forgatch, 1987).

46. Family meetings should use respectful communication skills such as taking turns talking, treating each other with respect, and no lecturing. (See page 118 of *Parents and Adolescents: Living Together. Vol II: Family Problem Solving* by Patterson and Forgatch, 1987).

47. Help parents establish consistent house rules for family meetings. Consequences for rule violation and compliance should be specified. Rules can be modified and negotiated in family meetings if necessary.

48. Help parents discuss the feasibility of family dinners, the frequency that dinners can occur, and the expectations for attendance by the adolescent.

49. Have parents meet with the adolescent (in session or as homework) to discuss and implement the family dinner plan at least once or twice a week.

—. _____

_____

—. _____

_____

—. _____

_____

DIAGNOSTIC SUGGESTIONS

Axis I	309.24	Adjustment Disorders With Anxiety
	309.0	Adjustment Disorders With Depressed Mood
	309.3	Adjustment Disorders With Disturbance of Conduct
	309.28	Adjustment Disorders With Mixed Anxiety and Depressed Mood
	309.4	Adjustment Disorders With Mixed Disturbance of Emotions and Conduct
	V61.21	Neglect of Child, 995.5 Victim
	V61.20	Parent-Child Relational Problem
	V61.1	Partner Relational Problem
	V61.1	Physical Abuse of Adult, 995.81 Victim
	V61.21	Physical Abuse of Child, 995.5 Victim
	V61.21	Sexual Abuse of Child, 995.5 Victim
	_____	_____
	_____	_____

PARENTING CONFLICTS—CHILDREN

BEHAVIORAL DEFINITIONS

1. Frequent arguments about parenting, or disagreements that interfere with effective child-rearing.
2. Lack of agreement between parents regarding strategies for dealing with various types of child misbehaviors.
3. Ineffective parental responses to child misbehavior (i.e., efforts do not result in the desired outcome).
4. Inability of partners to discuss and support each other's parenting efforts.

—. _____
   _____
—. _____
   _____
—. _____
   _____

LONG-TERM GOALS

1. Discuss and agree on the implementation of joint parenting strategies.

A more expansive description of the interventions summarized in this chapter can be found in Sanders (1992), Sanders and Dadds (1993), Sanders, Lynch and Markie-Dadds (1994), and Sanders, Markie-Dadds, and Nicholson (1997). An excellent overview of the overlap between relationship conflict and child behavior problems can be found in Cummings and Davies (1994).

2. Identify parenting and contextual factors that increase the frequency of child misbehavior.
3. Classify and respond to child misbehavior based on function.
4. Agree on the use of nonphysical means of dealing with serious child misbehavior.
5. Have daily casual conversations about parenting.
6. Create a positive, supportive parent-child home environment.
7. Discuss parenting strategies in a constructive manner on an ongoing basis.
8. Share ideas about parenting strategies and support each other's parenting behavior.

—. _____
   _____
   _____
—. _____
   _____
   _____
—. _____
   _____

SHORT-TERM OBJECTIVES

1. Discuss child problem behavior. (1, 2, 3, 4)
2. Identify the parenting and situational factors that may be maintaining the problem. (5, 6, 7)
3. Discuss how relationship functioning affects and is affected by parenting difficulties. (8, 9, 10, 27)
4. Define the motives for child's misbehavior—attention-seeking, escape or demand, or fun-seeking. (11)
5. State examples of child's misbehavior that are moti-

THERAPEUTIC INTERVENTIONS

1. Have parents describe their main concerns about child's problem behavior, and review its history. Therapist's questions might include: "When did problem behavior start?" and "How has it changed across time?"

2. Have parents specifically detail the extent of the child's problem behavior. Therapist's questions might include: "How frequently and intensely does problem behavior occur?" "How long does it last?" "In which situations does it occur?"

vated by attention-seeking. (12)

6. List examples of child's misbehavior that are motivated by escape or demand. (13)

7. Identify examples of child's misbehavior that are motivated by fun-seeking. (14)

8. Define a behavior in child that should be reinforced, and track its occurrence as well as antecedents and consequences. (15)

9. Identify a behavior in child that should be increased in frequency, and track its occurrence as well as antecedents and consequences. (16)

10. Track and identify the functions of the child's behaviors. (17)

11. Agree with partner to implement ignoring responses in reaction to attention-seeking behaviors by child. (18, 22)

12. Agree with partner to implement firm control in response to or escape demand behaviors of child. (19, 22)

13. Agree to implement commands and reprimands in response to fun-seeking behaviors by child. (20, 22)

14. List some natural and logical negative consequences (punishments) that could flow from specific misbehavior. (21, 22)

3. Identify specific child behavior and parenting problems by having parents complete questionnaire assessments such as the Child Behavior Checklist (Achenbach, 1991, 1992) and the Parenting Scale (Arnold, O'Leary, Wolff, and Acker, 1993).

4. Identify (*a*) each partner's parenting philosophy and strategy, and (*b*) each partner's expectations for the child's behavior (e.g., three-year-olds should sit through dinner quietly).

5. Identify parent-child behavioral patterns that may be maintaining the problem (e.g., unintentionally reinforcing problem behaviors, nattering, emotional parenting).

6. Identify social context factors that may be maintaining the problem (e.g., family transitions, inconsistent rules, school or social difficulties).

7. Identify parents' stressors that may be maintaining the problem (e.g., unemployment, substance use, depression).

8. Ask parents to indicate ways their relationship conflict has a negative impact on their child's behavior.

9. Have parents describe how their child's problem behav-

15. List ways to prevent some misbehaviors by anticipating them and planning ahead. (23)

16. Report instances of effectively employing time-out to deal with serious child misbehavior. (24)

17. Increase the frequency of contingently reinforcing positive child behavior. (25, 26)

18. Increase frequency of positive interactions with child. (27, 28)

19. Each parent identify, examine, and then pledge to terminate any negative behavior that he/she is modeling and that the child is imitating. (29)

20. Check with partner regularly concerning parenting and keep a log of these interactions. (30, 31, 32)

21. Use argument-control strategies to increase the productivity of parenting conversations. (33)

22. Report instances of constructive and supportive conversations with partner regarding current parenting experiences. (34, 35, 36)

23. Agree with partner to support each other's parenting. (37, 38, 39)

24. Regularly discuss and problem-solve parenting strategies for handling misbehavior. (40)

ior impacts on their relationship conflict.

10. Ask the partners to attempt to solve a major parenting problem. Quietly observe and note skills and deficiencies.

11. Educate parents regarding the three main motives for a child's misbehavior: attention-seeking, escape or demands, and fun-seeking.

12. Help parents identify examples of attention-seeking misbehavior (i.e., misbehavior that only occurs when someone is around, and for which the child secures attention prior to performing).

13. Help parents identify examples of demand-motivated misbehavior (i.e., misbehavior that promotes the child getting something he/she wants) and of escape-motivated misbehavior (i.e., misbehavior that promotes the child getting out of, or delaying, something he/she does not want to do).

14. Help parents identify examples of fun-motivated misbehavior (i.e., misbehavior that does not require someone to see it, and that the child attempts to hide).

15. Ask parents to select a child behavior that they would like to reinforce. Assign them to record its occurrence every day for a week,

25. Reach agreement with partner regarding the exact nature of a parenting problem before trying to resolve it. (40, 41, 42)

26. Agree with partner to discuss only one parenting problem at a time, and only after it has been pinpointed. (43)

27. Brainstorm with partner several possible parental interventions for the misbehavior. (44)

28. Evaluate with partner various possible solutions to the child's problematic behavior, choose one, and plan for its enactment and evaluation. (45, 46, 47)

29. Establish consistent house rules. (48)

—. _____
   _____

—. _____
   _____

—. _____
   _____

and to note the behaviors or situations that precede it (i.e., antecedents) and those that follow it (i.e., consequences).

16. Ask parents to select a behavior that they would like to discourage. Assign them to record its occurrence every day for a week, and to note the behaviors or situations that precede it (i.e., antecedents) and those that follow it (i.e., consequences).

17. After reviewing the parents' tracking sheets, have them identify the motives for each misbehavior observed (i.e., attention-seeking demand or escape, fun-seeking).

18. Role-play purposeful ignoring and encourage parents to use this technique to discourage attention-seeking misbehavior. Warn parents that inconsistent use of technique (e.g., ignoring misbehaviors some times but attending at other times) will only strengthen the misbehavior.

19. Help parents practice and troubleshoot firm, purposeful responses to demand/escape misbehavior.

20. Teach parents commands and reprimands to use in response to fun-motivated misbehavior. Responses should be firm, immediate, and brief, and they should

clearly state what behavior
is expected from the child.
Role-play implementation of
these commands.

21. Teach parents to establish
logical and natural consequences to child misbehavior (e.g., refuse to eat → go
hungry; make a mess →
clean up the mess).

22. Help parents formulate a
plan for appropriate,
function-based responses
to child misbehaviors
(e.g., attention = ignore,
demand/escape = do not
give in; fun = make the
behavior less fun).

23. Have parents list misbehavior situations that are consistently problematic. Help
them to identify the motivation for the misbehaviors
and to brainstorm ways of
preventing the misbehav-
iors (e.g., shorten duration
of shopping trips, pack
snacks for child).

24. Help parents practice and
troubleshoot responding to
serious misbehavior with
time-out technique (i.e.,
child sits in chair with no
attention for one to two
minutes per year of age).

25. Teach parents to notice and
reinforce child's positive
behaviors. Have each par-
ent practice behavior reinforcement in session, and
provide feedback.

26. Instruct parents in making "good behavior charts" (i.e., children earn points/tokens for appropriate behavior, and trade their points/tokens for things that they want).

27. Assign each parent to increase amount of focused, child-centered positive time with the child experiencing difficulty.

28. Assign each parent to increase number of casual, positive conversations with the child experiencing difficulty.

29. If parents are modeling for the child the behavior they would like to extinguish (e.g., yelling, hitting), have them contract to change their own behavior before trying to change the same behavior in the child.

30. Assign parents to confer with each other at least once a day regarding the child's behavior.

31. Encourage parents to plan a mutually acceptable time to confer, to avoid having casual conversations at times when arguments are likely to erupt (e.g., immediately upon arriving home in the evening).

32. Instruct partners to track their satisfaction with the daily check-ins and to bring in the tracking sheet to treatment sessions.

33. Assist partners in practicing argument control (e.g., partners calling time-out, using "I" messages in place of "you" messages). Assign partners to employ technique to cool off during parenting discussions if either believes the conversation is becoming unsupportive.

34. Help partners role-play discussions they will have when the children are well-behaved. Have the supportive partner ask the other what the children have been doing and then support his/her parenting behaviors.

35. Help partners role-play discussions they will have when the children are poorly behaved. Have the supportive partner ask, in a supportive, non-threatening manner, about the specifics of the misbehavior.

36. During role-playing exercises for dealing with child misbehavior, have the supportive partner ask in a supportive, nonthreatening manner about how the other dealt with the misbehavior and whether the supportive partner can do anything in the future to help.

37. Have partners contract to support each other's parenting by not interfering during the other's parent-child interactions, and by not interfering with the other's

decisions (i.e., avoiding splitting of parents' unity).

38. Help partners identify what each can do to help the other in challenging situations (e.g., play with or supervise the children while the other partner is on the phone).

39. Have partners contract to put disagreements over parenting strategy on hold until the situation has ended and they can meet privately, and both partners are calm and able to problem-solve without accusations or defensiveness.

40. Assign partners to schedule parenting problem-solving discussions for two or three times per week.

41. Help partners role-play using pinpointing skills to specifically identify the problem.

42. Help partners role-play the speaker-listener technique, where the listener does not respond with own thoughts until he/she has paraphrased the speaker's position to that person's satisfaction.

43. Advise partners to limit themselves to solving one problem at a time.

44. Encourage each partner to brainstorm at least two possible solutions to each of the child's problem behaviors.

45. Help partners role-play choosing a solution together

by judging the advantages and disadvantages of each possible solution.

46. Help partners plan together on how to enact solutions.

47. Have partners establish a time to review the progress of the solution, and to troubleshoot the solution as necessary.

48. Have parents discuss and establish consistent house rules.

__. _____

_____

__. _____

_____

__. _____

_____

DIAGNOSTIC SUGGESTIONS

Axis I	309.24	Adjustment Disorders With Anxiety
	309.0	Adjustment Disorders With Depressed Mood
	309.3	Adjustment Disorders With Disturbance of Conduct
	309.28	Adjustment Disorders With Mixed Anxiety and Depressed Mood
	309.4	Adjustment Disorders With Mixed Disturbance of Emotions and Conduct
	V61.21	Neglect of Child, 995.5 Victim
	V61.20	Parent-Child Relational Problem
	V61.1	Partner Relational Problem
	V61.1	Physical Abuse of Adult, 995.81 Victim
	V61.21	Physical Abuse of Child, 995.5 Victim
	V61.21	Sexual Abuse of Child, 995.5 Victim
	_____	_____
	_____	_____

PERSONALITY DIFFERENCES

BEHAVIORAL DEFINITIONS

1. One partner is introverted, whereas the other is extroverted.
2. One partner is assertive, whereas the other is passive.
3. One partner is gregarious, whereas the other prefers to be alone or only with partner.
4. One partner is religious, whereas the other is not.
5. One partner is physically active, whereas the other prefers sedentary activities.
6. One partner likes to listen to music, whereas the other does not.
7. One partner likes to watch sports, whereas the other does not.
8. One partner is independent, whereas the other is not.
9. Partners argue over choice of recreational activities.
10. One partner is much more moralistic than the other.
11. Communication is argumentative and/or avoidant.
12. Expressions of caring/love between partners have waned.

__. _____
   _____
__. _____
   _____
__. _____
   _____

LONG-TERM GOALS

1. Partners reach compromises that are acceptable to each.
2. One partner makes significant changes in style of relating.

3. Partners capitalize on their personality differences to enhance the relationship.
4. Partners accept certain personality differences and respect those differences.

—. _____
_____
—. _____
_____
—. _____
_____

SHORT-TERM OBJECTIVES

1. Describe own and partner's personality styles. (1, 2, 3, 4, 5)
2. Differentiate long-standing personality styles from recent habitual patterns. (3, 4, 5)
3. Describe personality differences that have enriched the relationship and make life more interesting. (6, 7, 8)
4. Verbalize how personality differences facilitate social functioning. (7)
5. Describe personality differences that have caused conflict in the relationship. (9, 10)
6. Agree to make some changes in habitual behavior. (11)
7. Agree to attempt changing a behavior that seems to represent a long-standing personality style. (12)

THERAPEUTIC INTERVENTIONS

1. Have each client develop a list of own personality styles that are similar to those of partner.
2. Help clients differentiate between habits (i.e., changeable behaviors) and personality styles (i.e., long-standing ways of approaching the world).
3. Ask each client to develop a list of own personality styles that differ significantly from those of partner.
4. Ask each client to develop a list of partner's important habits.
5. Ask each client to develop a list of own important habits.
6. Ask each client to describe how differences between self and partner enrich the relationship.
7. Help each client identify how differences between self and partner are valu-

8. Verbalize how personality differences in parents model very different behaviors for children. (13)

9. Verbalize acceptance of differences in personality styles between self and partner, and cite the value of some differences. (8, 14, 15, 16, 17)

10. Make positive comments to partner about the differences in personality styles. (18)

11. Make positive comments to family/friends about differences in personality styles. (19)

—. _____
   _____
—. _____
   _____
—. _____
   _____

able and help in social functioning.

8. Assist clients in understanding the value of differences in the relationship for intimate functioning.

9. Ask each client to describe how differences between self and partner are detrimental to the relationship.

10. Ask each client to describe how differences between self and partner are detrimental to social functioning.

11. Request that each partner identify and verbally commit to changing habitual patterns that are offensive to the other partner.

12. Request that each partner identify and verbally commit to changing behaviors that represent long-standing personality patterns and cause conflicts in the relationship.

13. Help clients understand the value of differences in the relationship for rearing children.

14. Assist clients in developing an understanding of the types of behavior that are very difficult to change.

15. Teach client about the types of personality styles that are very difficult to change.

16. Assist clients in accepting differences that can exist between them without any detriment to each other.

17. Educate clients regarding the value of their differences in personality.

18. Ask partners to make comments to each other in therapy session about the value of their differences.

19. Assign partners to make comments to family/friends about the value of their differences.

___. _____

_____

___. _____

_____

___. _____

_____

DIAGNOSTIC SUGGESTIONS

Axis I	309.0	Adjustment Disorder With Depressed Mood
	309.24	Adjustment Disorder With Anxiety
	309.28	Adjustment Disorder With Mixed Anxiety and Depressed Mood
	309.4	Adjustment Disorder With Mixed Disturbance of Emotions and Conduct
	309.3	Adjustment Disorders With Disturbance of Conduct
	V61.1	Partner Relational Problem
	_____	_____
	_____	_____
Axis II	301.7	Antisocial Personality Disorder
	301.83	Borderline Personality Disorder
	301.6	Dependent Personality Disorder
	301.50	Histrionic Personality Disorder
	301.4	Obsessive-Compulsive Personality Disorder
	301.81	Narcissistic Personality Disorder
	_____	_____
	_____	_____

PHYSICAL ABUSE

BEHAVIORAL DEFINITIONS

1. Intentional infliction of physical pain or injury on partner, or any action perceived by partner as having that intent (e.g., throwing objects at partner, pushing, grabbing, hitting, choking, extreme verbal sexual coercion, forced sex).
2. Intentional infliction of psychological pain or injury on partner, or any action perceived by partner as having that intent (e.g., damaging partner's prized possession, injury to pets, belittling partner, telling partner that he/she can't survive alone, monitoring partner's whereabouts, restricting partner's access to friends).
3. Partner's fear of continuing physical injury or emotional abuse resulting from assaultive acts, threats, intimidation, or berating by abusive partner.

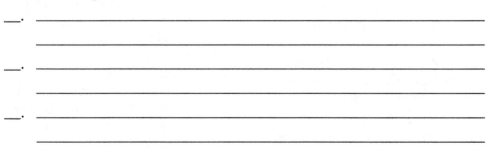

—. _____
_____
—. _____
_____
—. _____
_____

A more expansive description of the interventions summarized in this chapter can be found in Rosenbaum and O'Leary (1986) and Vivian and Heyman (1996). Therapists should be cautioned to throughly understand the controversies and contraindications of conjoint approaches to abuse (see Heyman and Schlee, in press; O'Leary, 1996; McMahon and Pence, 1996) before attempting to use the suggestions summarized in this chapter.

LONG-TERM GOALS

1. Eliminate all physical aggression in the relationship.
2. Establish safety plan for victim (i.e., concrete plan detailing cues for danger and steps that will be taken to enhance safety).
3. Eliminate all emotional abuse and coercion in the relationship.
4. Examine the pros and cons of remaining in the relationship.

—. _____

_____

—. _____

_____

—. _____

_____

SHORT-TERM OBJECTIVES

1. Both partners agree to attend individual and/or conjoint sessions as directed by the therapist. (1)

2. If either partner has committed acts of physical or psychological abuse, he/she agrees to sign a nonviolence, nonintimidation contract. (2, 3, 4)

3. Both partners verbalize behavioral definitions of physical and psychological abuse. (5)

4. Victim of abuse verbalizes a plan for avoidance or escape if violence erupts or becomes imminent. (3, 6, 7)

5. Both partners identify the behaviors that typically signal the escalation toward violence. (8, 9, 10)

THERAPEUTIC INTERVENTIONS

1. In individual sessions, determine the appropriateness of conjoint versus individual treatment by assessing the current context of partner abuse. Factors to be considered include: (*a*) antecedents, (*b*) impact, (*c*) function, (*d*) fear, (*e*) safety issues, (*f*) extent of psychological coercion or abuse, (*g*) openness to discuss issues dyadically, and (*h*) resistance to disclose or discuss violence. Recommend to the couple whether conjoint or individual therapy is indicated.

2. Have both partners sign a contract stipulating that no abusive behavior will occur, even when feeling angry.

6. Both partners agree to use time out to defuse a situation when anger-escalating behaviors begin. (8, 9, 10, 11)

7. Both partners agree not to use in-session material as a weapon outside of the session. (12)

8. Both partners agree to abide by the therapist's directions if the session process becomes destructive. (13)

9. Both partners cooperate openly with a substance abuse evaluation. (14)

10. Both partners verbalize an understanding of their core beliefs that sustain the pattern of violence. (15, 16)

11. Both partners verbalize negative effects of partner abuse on victim, abuser, and children. (17, 18)

12. Aggressive partner accepts responsibility for abusive behaviors and verbally commits to not blame other partner for inciting abuse. (10, 19, 20)

13. Aggressive partner writes a plan that provides several alternatives to abusive behavior when anger is triggered. (21, 22, 23, 24, 25)

14. Aggressive partner apologizes for abusive behavior, naming the behaviors and taking full responsibility for them. (26)

15. Victim holds aggressive partner responsible for the

3. Establish plan for what each partner will do if non-violence contract is violated (e.g., call police, leave the situation, arrange for separation).

4. Educate both partners that partner abuse is illegal and maladaptive.

5. Assist the couple in defining physical and emotional abuse in concrete, behavior terms.

6. Refer victim to victim services, and refer aggressive partner to abusers' group treatment, if (*a*) victim is fearful, (*b*) severe abuse occurs, or (*c*) emotional or physical well-being of victim is jeopardized.

7. Establish a safety plan for victim (i.e., identification of violence cues and resources for assistance; prearrangement of items necessary for escape, such as extra car keys and escape money; and a plan of where to go and what to do if violence erupts).

8. Teach partners to recognize the gradations of anger and the behaviors and cognitions associated with it.

9. Train partners to recognize and label emotions other than anger, and to identify emotions that often precede anger.

10. Assign anger-tracking homework that identifies

abuse while accepting an apology for the abuse. (27)

16. Aggressive partner reports instances where feelings of anger were expressed in a controlled, assertive, respectful manner. (23, 24, 28)

17. Aggressive partner identifies childhood experiences with violence and verbal abuse that taught him/her the acceptability of abusive behavior. (29)

18. Victim identifies childhood experiences that taught him/her that abusive behavior is to be expected, excused, and tolerated. (30)

19. Victim identifies pattern of blaming self for the abusive behavior of the partner. (31)

20. Victim reports instances when aggressive or abusive behavior occurred and he/she did not verbalize being at fault for it. (28, 31, 32)

21. Aggressive partner identifies instances of being a childhood victim of abuse and shares the feelings of pain, helplessness, and rage these experiences generated. (33, 34)

22. Aggressive partner verbalizes feelings of inadequacy, failure, and fear that fuel the anger. (9, 10, 33, 34)

23. Aggressive partner verbalizes an understanding of the need for forgiveness of

the situations that trigger anger as well as the thoughts and behaviors that occur during anger-eliciting situations.

11. Using role-playing, modeling, and behavior rehearsal, teach the six components of time-out technique (i.e., *self-monitoring* for escalating feelings of anger and hurt, *signaling* to partner that verbal engagement should end, *acknowledging* the need of partner to disengage, *separating* to disengage, *cooling down* to regain control of anger, and *returning* to controlled verbal engagement).

12. Educate partners regarding the negative impact on the therapy process of being critical or angry with other partner for what he/she says in a session.

13. Educate partners regarding the need for each to respect the other in sessions, especially when feelings become strong. Emphasize the therapist's responsibility for maintaining control of the session and for interrupting destructive patterns of interaction.

14. Assess clients for the presence of chemical dependence in either partner and for its contribution to the abusive behavior pattern.

others and self to begin to reduce anger. (35, 36)

24. Both partners identify negative communication patterns that facilitate aggression. (37)

25. Both partners role-play situations wherein they can practice positive communication skills. (38)

—. _____
_____

—. _____
_____

—. _____
_____

15. Renegotiate the partners' existing unhealthy, dysfunctional, implicit relationship contract (i.e., who has right to do what?) into a contract that calls for mutual respect for individual opinions, beliefs, and feelings.

16. Identify and challenge gender-based beliefs that promote abuse (e.g., that women are inferior, men have ultimate authority, women deserve abuse when they do not comply with men's wishes).

17. Have each partner describe history of psychological and/or physical victimization in childhood.

18. Educate clients regarding the destructive consequences that partner abuse has (or can have) on each partner and upon their children.

19. Confront aggressive partner's tendency to excuse own abusive behavior by blaming partner for provoking it.

20. Model the taking of responsibility for behavior, and reinforce each partner's acceptance of full responsibility for his/her behavioral decisions.

21. Educate partners regarding the differences between nonassertive, assertive, and aggressive communication.

22. Establish for partners the function of partner abuse,

and identify nonabusive means to accomplish such goals.

23. Process recent examples of aggressive partner's angry feelings or angry outbursts and review alternative behaviors that were available.

24. Assign aggressive partner to list several alternative behaviors to abuse when anger is felt (e.g., taking time out, calling a friend, taking a walk, writing out feelings, reviewing list of negative consequences of violence).

25. Assign aggressive partner to read *Of Course You're Angry* (Rosellini and Worden, 1986) or *The Angry Book* (Rubin, 1969).

26. Confront aggressive partner regarding the need for him/her to take responsibility for the abuse and to express remorse.

27. Confront victim's pattern of taking responsibility for aggressive partner's behavior decisions, and reinforce victim for holding aggressive partner responsible for the abusive behavior.

28. Reinforce assertive behaviors in session and reports of successful assertiveness between sessions.

29. Review with aggressive partner previous life experi-

ences that taught him/her that violence and verbal abuse are acceptable behaviors for expressing anger.

30. Review with victim previous life experiences that taught him/her that violence and verbal abuse are behaviors that are to be expected, excused, and tolerated.

31. Help victim identify a pattern of blaming self for partner's abusive behavior, and teach him/her personal responsibility for behavioral decisions.

32. Reinforce victim for holding aggressive partner responsible for aggressive behavior.

33. Assign aggressive partner to list hurtful life experiences that have led to anger.

34. Empathize with and clarify feelings of hurt and anger tied to traumas of past.

35. Discuss victim's forgiveness of aggressive partner for pain as a process of "letting go" of anger.

36. Assign aggressive partner to read *Forgive and Forget* (Smedes, 1991).

37. Identify negative communication patterns in relationship that accompany and/or increase the likelihood of physical aggression (e.g., vocally blaming partner for problems; fast reciprocation

of partner's anger; lack of empathy; contempt for or lack of respect for partner; defensiveness; refusal to change; resistance; withdrawal; coercive control/ entitlement).

38. Using role-playing and behavior rehearsal, teach partners positive communication skills (e.g., problem identification, "I" statements, listening skills, problem-solving skills, behavioral contracting) and assign practice as homework.

___. _____

_____

___. _____

_____

___. _____

_____

DIAGNOSIS SUGGESTIONS

Axis I	309.0	Adjustment Disorder With Depressed Mood
	309.24	Adjustment Disorder With Anxiety
	309.28	Adjustment Disorder With Mixed Anxiety and Depressed Mood
	309.4	Adjustment Disorder With Mixed Disturbance of Emotions and Conduct
	309.3	Adjustment Disorders With Disturbance of Conduct
	305.00	Alcohol Abuse
	303.90	Alcohol Dependence
	300.4	Dysthymic Disorder
	296.x	Major Depressive Disorder
	V61.1	Partner Relational Problem

	V61.1	Physical Abuse of Adult, 995.81 Victim
	309.81	Posttraumatic Stress Disorder
	‾‾‾	_____
	‾‾‾	_____
Axis II	301.7	Antisocial Personality Disorder
	301.83	Borderline Personality Disorder
	301.6	Dependent Personality Disorder
	301.50	Histrionic Personality Disorder
	301.4	Obsessive-Compulsive Personality Disorder
	301.81	Narcissistic Personality Disorder
	‾‾‾	_____
	‾‾‾	_____

PSYCHOLOGICAL ABUSE

BEHAVIORAL DEFINITIONS

1. Insults partner when alone and in front of others.
2. Swears at partner.
3. Calls partner demeaning, degrading names (e.g., lazy, sloppy).
4. Makes critical, demeaning comments about partner's body (e.g., fat, bald, ugly, skinny).
5. Makes critical and demeaning comments about partner's ability to perform his/her job.
6. Makes critical comments about partner's ability to perform roles in home (e.g., cook, fix things, clean, take care of yard).
7. Accuses partner, without cause, of sexual promiscuity and infidelity.
8. Makes critical comments about partner's sexuality or sexual performance.
9. Makes critical statement about partner's mental health (e.g., "You are crazy," "You need a psychiatrist," "You are paranoid").
10. Threatens to do physical harm to partner.
11. Threatens to leave partner.
12. Threatens to have sex with someone else.
13. Tries to prevent partner from having contact with friends and family.
14. Tries to prevent partner from leaving home.
15. Prevents partner from using car (e.g., takes keys; removes spark plugs or wires).
16. Refuses to talk to partner for days (i.e., silent treatment).
17. Makes partner account for time.
18. Jealous of partner's time spent with other individuals (especially of opposite sex).
19. Discourages partner from obtaining further training or education that would enhance his/her self-esteem and opportunities for advancement.

20. Orders partner around in a dominating, controlling, and belittling manner.

—. _____
_____
—. _____
_____
—. _____
_____

LONG-TERM GOALS

1. Terminate verbal and/or psychological abuse and establish a relationship based in respect and a desire for mutual enhancement.
2. Replace hostile, threatening, and critical comments with respectful communication that builds self-esteem.
3. Eliminate threats to leave the relationship and/or to have sex with others.
4. Eliminate the use of controlling behaviors that attempt to keep partner physically nearby and away from friends and family.
5. Eliminate the use of controlling behaviors that attempt to keep partner from bettering herself/himself.
6. Evaluate alternatives to current relationship.

—. _____
_____
—. _____
_____
—. _____
_____

SHORT-TERM OBJECTIVES

1. Verbalize agreement to stop hostile comments and name-calling. (1, 2, 3)
2. Identify partner's comments that are especially damaging to self-esteem. (4, 5)

THERAPEUTIC INTERVENTIONS

1. Obtain verbal commitment from partners not to engage in name-calling or making hostile comments.
2. Advise partners of the need for individual therapy if

3. Verbalize an understanding of the negative impact of abuse. (6, 7)

4. Verbally agree not to use psychological coercion or threat of physical force to obtain sexual interaction. (8, 9)

5. Identify the negative consequences of using coercion for sexual activity. (10, 11)

6. Terminate threats to have sex with someone else. (12)

7. Terminate threats to leave partner. (13)

8. Terminate all threats of physical aggression against the partner for any reason. (14)

9. Describe instances of coercion or threats of physical violence in the relationship. (15)

10. Abused, fearful partner accepts a referral to a safe environment. (17)

11. Verbalize an understanding of male control and misuse of power in our society. (18, 19, 20)

12. Both partners agree to build each other's self esteem through compliments, appreciation, and acts of kindness. (21)

13. Agree to accept and encourage contact by both partners with friends and family as a means of improving the relationship. (22)

anger cannot be controlled in the conjoint therapy sessions.

3. Discuss with partners the need for both to be psychologically ready before conjoint therapy is indicated, and to accept responsibility for minimizing any major negative events that might occur in therapy.

4. Have each client describe comments by partner that hurt him/her the most.

5. Have each partner describe the areas of own life where he/she feels most vulnerable.

6. Using role-reversal technique, have abusive partner assume abused partner's identity and then identify the emotional impact of the abusive behavior.

7. Confront any displays of or references to abusive behavior, and educate clients regarding its destructive consequences.

8. Obtain commitment from partners not to use physical force to coerce sexual interaction.

9. Educate clients that to have a positive sexual relationship, the sexual activity must be acceptable to both partners.

10. Educate clients that pressure by one partner to engage in sexual activity usually leads to sexual aversions and/or avoidance

14. Agree to support each other in obtaining training or education. (23)

15. Abusive partner identifies fears that motivate controlling behavior. (24)

16. List the negative consequences of exerting control over other partner. (25)

17. Demonstrate respectful, accurate communication with partner. (26, 27)

18. Assess alternatives to the relationship and accept referrals regarding respite from the relationship. (28, 29, 30)

19. Both partners agree to minimize negative relationship interactions in the presence of their children. (31, 32)

___. _____
_____
___. _____
_____
___. _____
_____

and dislike by the other partner.

11. Educate clients that sexual behavior is one of the most sensitive of all human behaviors, and that aversive control by one partner can quickly lead to disinterest and sexual dysfunction in the other partner.

12. Obtain verbal commitment from partners not to threaten to have sex with someone else.

13. Obtain verbal commitment from partners not to threaten to leave the relationship during term of therapy. An agreement about the length of therapy should be developed at the beginning of treatment.

14. Obtain verbal commitment from clients not to engage in any physical force against the partner for any reason. Be aware that when intense verbal intimidation exists, the risk for physical aggression also is high.

15. Ask both partners to describe the extent to which psychological coercion and threats of violence are present in the relationship in general.

16. Ask both partners to describe the perceived or experienced negative consequences of threatened violence.

17. If the abused partner's fear of violence is intense, pro-

vide a referral to a safe
environment (e.g., battered-
women's shelters, abuse
hot-line numbers).

18. Review and discuss with
partners the role of patriarchy in American society.

19. Review and discuss with
clients how the controlling
partner misuses his/her
power.

20. Educate clients regarding
how controlling behaviors
by one partner lead to dislike and avoidance by the
other partner.

21. Review with clients the evidence regarding the association between psychological
aggression and poor self-
esteem and/or depression.
Have clients list specific
ways for them to build self-
esteem in each other.

22. Educate clients regarding
the fact that external social
support (e.g., contact with
friends) and relationship
satisfaction are positively
related.

23. Educate clients regarding
the need for each partner to
be able to venture out from
the relationship with the
sense that the other will be
supportive of him/her (i.e.,
for bettering self through
education or training or job
enhancement).

24. Have abusive partner identify the feelings (e.g., jealousy, fears of inadequacy)

that underlie the need for controlling behavior of either partner.

25. Assist partners in listing the negative consequences of controlling behavior on the abused partner (e.g., resentment, avoidance, waning of caring feelings).

26. Have each partner listen to the other about a relationship matter without interrupting, and then paraphrase what the other said.

27. Provide feedback and interpretation to partners about their communication styles.

28. In an individual session with the psychologically abused client, have him/her evaluate the available alternatives to the current relationship.

29. Suggest reading materials for abused client, such as *The Verbally Abusive Relationship* (Evans, 1996).

30. If necessary, refer psychologically abused client to an agency for battered women and/or to a shelter.

31. If clients have children, review with partners the evidence showing a significant link between open hostility between parents and psychopathology in children (i.e., increased incidence of conduct problems and anxiety problems).

32. If the partners have children, have both partners

commit to minimizing negative interactions in the
presence of the children.

__. _____

_____

__. _____

_____

__. _____

_____

DIAGNOSTIC SUGGESTIONS

Axis I:	309.0	Adjustment Disorder With Depressed Mood
	309.24	Adjustment Disorder With Anxiety
	309.28	Adjustment Disorder With Mixed Anxiety and Depressed Mood
	309.4	Adjustment Disorder With Mixed Disturbance of Emotions and Conduct
	309.3	Adjustment Disorders With Disturbance of Conduct
	305.00	Alcohol Abuse
	303.90	Alcohol Dependence
	300.4	Dysthymic Disorder
	296.x	Major Depressive Disorder
	V61.1	Partner Relational Problem
	V61.1	Physical Abuse of Adult, 995.81 Victim
	309.81	Posttraumatic Stress Disorder
	_____	_____
Axis II:	301.7	Antisocial Personality Disorder
	301.83	Borderline Personality Disorder
	301.6	Dependent Personality Disorder
	301.50	Histrionic Personality Disorder
	301.4	Obsessive-Compulsive Personality Disorder
	301.81	Narcissistic Personality Disorder
	_____	_____
	_____	_____

RECREATIONAL ACTIVITIES DISPUTE

BEHAVIORAL DEFINITIONS

1. Conflict over choice of leisure activities to be shared by partners.
2. Conflict over time spent by one partner in his/her individual recreational activities.
3. Uncomfortable feelings of disconnectedness due to one or both partners engaging extensively in separate, unshared recreational activities.
4. Disagreement over the manner in which vacation time is spent.
5. Erosion of quality or quantity of time spent in partner-pleasing activities.

LONG-TERM GOALS

1. Identify and plan regular positive activities, to be enjoyed both alone and together.
2. Discuss and respect each other's varying interests.
3. Find opportunities to enjoy elements of each other's hobbies or interests as a means of giving of self to the other partner.
4. Plan vacation opportunities in a manner that maximizes mutual enjoyment and minimizes conflict.

—. _____
   _____
   _____

—. _____
   _____
   _____

—. _____
   _____

SHORT-TERM OBJECTIVES

1. Verbally define current level of satisfaction with recreational activities. (1, 2)

2. Generate lists of recreational activities that each partner would like to do alone, with partner, or with others. (3)

3. Identify interests that are shared with partner and those that are unique to each partner. (4)

4. Discuss and listen in a respectful manner to other partner's leisure-time likes and dislikes. (5, 6)

5. Identify and plan pleasurable activities of varying lengths. (7, 8, 9)

6. Discuss the impact of planned pleasurable activities and contract for continued weekly planning. (11, 12)

7. Each partner identify an activity that is primarily enjoyable to the other partner that he/she can occasionally show an interest in or participate in. (10, 14, 15)

THERAPEUTIC INTERVENTIONS

1. Identify each partner's level of satisfaction with recreational activities that are done (a) individually and (b) as a couple.

2. Ask each partner to identify elements of recreational activities that he/she believes are in need of improvement (i.e., frequency, quality, particular activities).

3. Ask partners to complete the Inventory of Rewarding Activities (Birchler and Weiss, 1977) to generate a list of desired activities in the following categories: (a) to do alone, (b) to do with partner, (c) to do with partner and other family members, (d) to do with partner and nonfamily members, and (e) to do with nonfamily members.

4. Have partners discuss the similarities and differences of their lists.

5. For important activities about which partners dis-

8. Negotiate an agreement that allows each partner some time to pursue an activity that is pleasurable to him/her while being considerate in not allowing the activity to dominate the couple's available free time. (16, 17)

9. Use problem-solving skills to find agreement on how both partners can enjoy a vacation site. (18, 19)

10. Show respect for each other's vacation interests by agreeing to spend equal time together at one partner's choice, followed by time together at other partner's choice. (20)

11. Bring joy to each other's lives by planning and periodically implementing a high-intensity day of positive activities that focus alternately on each partner's wishes. (21, 22)

__. _____
_____
__. _____
_____
__. _____
_____

agree, have partners discuss their points of view by taking turns as speakers. For example, "When I go hunting, I feel alive and part of nature."

6. After the speaker states his/her preferences, have the listener show respect for the other's point of view by paraphrasing it and by refraining from criticism.

7. Assign each client to independently list 5 to 10 activities or behaviors that he/she could do that the other partner would enjoy.

8. Have each person classify the partner-enjoyable activities into those that can be done in 15–30 minutes, 1–2 hours, 4–6 hours, a full day, and a weekend.

9. Have clients use their lists of rewarding activities to schedule one week's activities (e.g., work, responsibilities, chores, and leisure pursuits).

10. Assign clients to join in or arrange for their partner at least three activities that are enjoyable for the partner (scaled to fit their time demands) per week; have clients record the activity and rate the quality of satisfaction.

11. Ask each partner to discuss the week's pleasurable activity assignment using "I" statements. For example, "When we went for a walk

at the beach this weekend, I felt really peaceful and close to you. I'd like us to go for a walk at least once a weekend in the future." Have the listener respond using paraphrasing and reflecting skills.

12. After reviewing and troubleshooting pleasurable activity assignment, have clients contract to schedule their activities weekly.

13. If one partner does not share an interest in the other's hobby (e.g., one plays golf and the other does not), have him/her brainstorm ways to share in the other's pleasure (e.g., go to the club and read while partner plays; ask the partner about golf round when he/she returns home).

14. Encourage each partner to commit to occasionally and sacrificially showing an interest or participating in an activity (e.g., attending a symphony concert) that is pleasurable to the other partner but not to self.

15. Have partners contract to respect each other's interests and hobbies by not criticizing the other's hobby or other enjoyable activity.

16. Have partners contract to respect each other by not letting any one activity or hobby dominate own free time.

17. Have partners contract to respect each other's interests and hobbies by scheduling time each week for mutually-enjoyable and individually-enjoyable leisure activities.

18. If partners disagree on vacation sites (e.g., one likes the beach and the other does not), help them brainstorm ways in which they can still enjoy mutual destinations (e.g., one goes to the beach while the other shops in nearby town).

19. If partners disagree on vacation sites, help them brainstorm ways to include others and thereby increase the attractiveness of the partner's preferred site (e.g., vacationing with another family to provide each partner with company to share favorite pursuits).

20. If partners disagree on vacation sites, help them brainstorm ways to make destination choices equitable (e.g., one summer go to the beach, the next to the mountains).

21. Have partners plan a "love day" periodically, during which one partner receives from the other partner as many beneficial activities (especially benefits that don't occur on typical days) as possible. For example, a husband might give his wife a backrub, take care of the

children while she exercises, and then prepare a romantic, candlelight dinner.

22. Ask partners to alternate who will be the recipient of "love day" and who will be the giver.

__. _____
   _____
__. _____
   _____
__. _____
   _____

DIAGNOSTIC SUGGESTIONS

Axis I	309.0	Adjustment Disorder With Depressed Mood
	309.24	Adjustment Disorder With Anxiety
	309.28	Adjustment Disorder With Mixed Anxiety and Depressed Mood
	305.00	Alcohol Abuse
	303.90	Alcohol Dependence
	300.4	Dysthymic Disorder
	300.02	Generalized Anxiety Disorder
	296.x	Major Depressive Disorder
	300.21	Panic Disorder With Agoraphobia
	V61.1	Partner Relational Problem
	_____	_____
	_____	_____

RELIGION/SPIRITUALITY DIFFERENCES

BEHAVIORAL DEFINITIONS

1. Upsetting verbal disagreements between partners over religious faith (i.e., core beliefs about life and afterlife) and practices (e.g., communal worship, prayer).
2. Attempts by one partner to coerce other into accepting own religious and spiritual beliefs, values, or activities.
3. Reduced intimacy between partners due to inability to constructively share deeply held core beliefs and values.
4. Conflicts between partners about their children's religious training and expected attendance at worship services.
5. Arguments between partners over proper child-discipline strategies, fueled at least in part by differing religious and spiritual beliefs about parenting.

—. _____
   _____
—. _____
   _____
—. _____
   _____

LONG-TERM GOALS

1. Recognize developmental changes in religious beliefs and/or changes in tolerance about the partner's religious and spiritual beliefs, values, or activities.

2. Commit selves to strengthening the relationship by: (*a*) identifying advantages of each other's beliefs, (*b*) respecting each other's views, and (*c*) accommodating each other's practices.
3. Increase intimacy of relationship by discussing core beliefs and existential meaning.
4. Agree to work together in parental roles of religious instruction and discipline.

—. _____
_____
—. _____
_____
—. _____
_____

SHORT-TERM OBJECTIVES

1. Verbally trace the developmental history of each partner's religious and spiritual beliefs. (1, 2)
2. Identify the impact of each partner's religious beliefs on the relationship. (3, 4)
3. Discuss the history of and reasons for current conflict over religious and spiritual beliefs. (5, 6, 7)
4. Each partner identify how his/her religious and spiritual beliefs strengthen the relationship. (8)
5. Each partner identify how couple's religious differences cause conflict in other areas of the relationship. (9)
6. Promise respect for other partner's religious and spiritual beliefs, values or activ-

THERAPEUTIC INTERVENTIONS

1. Ask each partner to identify the role that religion and spirituality played in his/her childhood home and family experience.
2. Have partners trace changes that have taken place in their religious and spiritual beliefs, values, or activities as they have grown older.
3. Ask partners to discuss the role that religious and spiritual beliefs played in their lives during the early stages of their relationship.
4. Ask partners to discuss the meaning of marriage in their respective religious and spiritual belief systems.
5. Identify ways that partners' religious and spiritual

ities, and agree not to coerce other partner into belief conformity. (10, 11)

7. Share the meaning of commitment, respect, intimacy, forgiveness, and sexuality within each partner's religious and spiritual belief system. (12, 14)

8. Share how the meaning of commitment, respect, intimacy, forgiveness, and sexuality within each partner's religious and spiritual belief system is evidenced within the relationship. (13, 14)

9. Each partner articulate own core beliefs, including the meaning of human existence. (15)

10. Each partner share how own core beliefs have helped to provide meaning to his/her personal life. (16)

11. Verbalize how religious beliefs and practice are important for support of core beliefs. (17)

12. Demonstrate respect for the other partner's professed religious and spiritual beliefs by engaging in listener behaviors that facilitate the free exchange of views regarding the meaning of human existence. (18, 19, 20)

13. Verbalize reasons why it is important to self that other partner agree in religious beliefs and practice; then offer constructive ways to

beliefs, values, or activities have changed since they met.

6. Identify when partners' conflict over religious and spiritual beliefs, values, or activities began.

7. Ask partners to describe when and how they argue or disagree about religious and spiritual beliefs, values, and activities.

8. Ask each client to describe ways in which his/her religious and spiritual beliefs, values, and activities strengthen the relationship.

9. Ask each client to describe the ways in which religious and spiritual differences accentuate conflict in other areas of the relationship (e.g., role strain, parenting).

10. Have clients contract to respect each other's religious and spiritual beliefs by not criticizing the other's beliefs, values, or activities.

11. Have clients contract to respect each other's religious and spiritual beliefs by agreeing not to coerce the other into conforming to self's beliefs, values, or activities.

12. Ask each partner to discuss the values placed on (*a*) commitment, (*b*) respect, (*c*) intimacy, and (*d*) forgiveness within the framework of his/her religious and/or spiritual belief system.

respond to ongoing disagreement. (21)

14. Identify the degree of flexibility available for accommodating divergent beliefs. (22, 23, 24)

15. List the perceived advantages and disadvantages of belief-based community social activities. (25)

16. Each partner verbalize own need to socialize with others in his/her religious community, and indicate the extent to which he/she would like partner to participate in this socialization. (26)

17. Verbalize any explicit agreements that were made regarding the children's religious training before they were born and the current feelings about those agreements. (27, 28)

18. Each partner state his/her current wishes for the religious training of the children. (29)

19. Reach agreement on children's religious training that each partner can accept and support. (30)

20. Identify the effects that partners' religious and spiritual differences have on parenting. (31, 32)

21. Agree on a parenting philosophy and behaviors that each partner can accept and support. (33)

13. Have each partner discuss how the values placed on (a) commitment, (b) respect, (c) intimacy, and (d) forgiveness provide evidence of his/her religious and or spiritual belief.

14. Help partners identify the impact that their differing religious and spiritual beliefs have on their sexual relationship.

15. Help each partner identify own core beliefs (e.g., the existence and nature of God, the nature of man, the meaning of human life, the existence and nature of an afterlife) and how he/she came to that belief system.

16. Have each partner consider and share the ways that religious and spiritual beliefs have added meaning to his/her personal life.

17. Have each partner consider and share the ways that religious and spiritual beliefs and practices reinforce his/her core beliefs.

18. Ask the listening partner to show respect for the speaker's beliefs by paraphrasing the speaker's beliefs, even if he/she does not agree with the speaker.

19. Ask the listening partner to show respect for the speaker's beliefs by not responding with lecturing or preaching, even if he/she does not agree with the speaker.

—. _____
   _____
—. _____
   _____
—. _____
   _____

20. Ask the listening partner to show respect for the speaker's beliefs by not arguing against the speaker's beliefs.

21. Allow each client who so desires to describe (a) why it is important for him/her that the other partner accept and adopt his/her religious beliefs, and (b) how he/she will constructively cope with a lack of agreement between them.

22. Help each partner identify what deviations from core beliefs he/she can accommodate or tolerate in the other partner.

23. Help each partner identify what deviations from core beliefs he/she cannot accommodate or tolerate in the other partner.

24. Have each partner identify his/her core belief regarding divorce.

25. Have both partners address the advantages and disadvantages of the sense of community brought to the relationship by either partner's religious and spiritual activities.

26. Ask each partner to identify and verbalize the perceived need for social support from his/her religious and spiritual community, and seek agreement as to the other partner's cooperative participation in that social network.

27. If the couple has children, identify whether an explicit agreement regarding their religious training was reached prior to their birth.

28. If either partner has misgivings about the original agreement about the children's religious upbringing, have him/her verbalize that position using nonblaming "I" statements.

29. Have each partner verbalize his/her current expectations for the children's religious instruction or practice.

30. Help partners to brainstorm agreements regarding their children's religious instruction and practice that both partners can abide by.

31. If the couple has children, identify whether either's religious and/or spiritual beliefs guide his/her approach to discipline.

32. If religious and spiritual beliefs guide either partner's parenting practices, have both discuss the strengths and conflicts arising from that approach.

33. Help partners to brainstorm ways in which strengths can be maintained and conflicts reduced from their religious and/or spiritually guided parenting practices.

—. _____

_____

___.   _____
      _____
___.   _____
      _____

DIAGNOSIS SUGGESTIONS

Axis I: V61.1   Partner Relational Problem

             _____   _____

             _____   _____

SEPARATION AND DIVORCE

BEHAVIORAL DEFINITIONS

1. Thoughts about ending the marriage (or the relationship, if not married).
2. Moving out of the home to establish separate living arrangements due to dissatisfaction with the relationship.
3. Initiation of legal proceedings for separation, divorce and/or child custody.
4. Confusion about how to best deal with the feelings and welfare of the children.
5. Anger, hurt, and fear regarding breaking the partnership and having to face life as a single person.
6. Spiritual conflict over the breaking of marriage vows.
7. Depression and withdrawal as a part of the grief process related to the loss of the relationship.

—. _____
_____
—. _____
_____
—. _____
_____

LONG-TERM GOALS

1. Evaluate the possibility of resolving the differences and review the pros and cons of remaining married.

2. Consistently uphold "the best interests of the children" as paramount and act accordingly, regardless of the final fate of the marriage.
3. Resolve the initial confusion and turmoil of separation.
4. Learn to cope with the varied losses that separation entails.
5. Mourn the end of the marriage adequately to facilitate cooperation in reaching a fair divorce agreement.
6. Reduce conflict, hurt, and angry feelings between partners.
7. Establish and maintain healthy coparenting practices.
8. Rediscover affectionate feelings and renew commitment to each other to work toward resolution of conflicts.

—. _____
   _____
—. _____
   _____
—. _____
   _____

SHORT-TERM OBJECTIVES

1. Each partner verbalize facts and feelings regarding own emotional stability, physical health, vocational satisfaction, and any religious conflicts regarding divorce. (1)
2. If significant emotional, medical, or vocational problems predate the serious relationship conflicts, agree to postpone the divorce or separation decision until the other issues have been resolved. (2)
3. Verbally acknowledge that there is no interest in conjoint or individual counseling to improve the marriage

THERAPEUTIC INTERVENTIONS

1. Assess each partner's emotional health, physical health, vocational stability, and religious conflict over divorce.
2. If significant extramarital problems exist, encourage each partner to postpone the decision about separation until after those problems have been addressed.
3. Establish the type of treatment that will be conducted, by describing and having partners agree to (a) conjoint marital therapy, (b) individual marital treatment, or (c) predivorce treatment.

but only interest in predivorce treatment. (3)

4. Cooperate with psychological testing to assess the
degree of acceptance of the
decision to divorce. (4)

5. Describe the origination,
development, and present
state of the relationship.
(5, 6, 7)

6. Describe any suspicions
regarding the other partner
having had an affair. (8)

7. Verbalize any incidents of
physical, sexual, or emo-
tional abuse or intimidation
by other partner. (9)

8. List the members of each
partner's extended family
who have broken committed
relationships, and discuss
the impact that this history
may have on a decision to
divorce. (10)

9. Identify any cultural, ethnic,
or religious beliefs that may
have a bearing on a decision
to divorce. Verbalize a resolution of such conflicts. (11)

10. Each partner identify how
he/she behaved in ways that
improved the relationship,
and how he/she behaved in
ways that harmed the relationship. (12)

11. List the pros and cons of the
available options—continuing the relationship, separation, and divorce. (13)

12. Verbalize empathy for each
other while each partner
states how divorce will

4. Assess the steps each partner has taken toward
divorce by administering
the Marital Status Inven-
tory (Weiss and Cerreto,
1980) and interviewing each
partner about his/her sense
of hope and vision of the
future.

5. Assess the developmental
stage of the marriage (i.e.,
early marriage, couple with
young children, long-term
marriage).

6. Assess the history of the
marriage (e.g., recent
changes in respective partners' happiness with relationship, their expectations
for the marriage, and
thoughts about divorce).

7. Assess partners' current
satisfaction with relationship, using interview and
self-report instruments
(e.g., Relationship Satisfaction Questionnaire by
Burns, 1984; Marital
Adjustment Test by Locke
and Wallace, 1959; or
Dyadic Adjustment Scale by
Spanier, 1976).

8. Assess the presence or suspicion of affairs in relationship (see Infidelity and
Jealousy chapters of this
Planner).

9. Assess for incidents of violence or intimidation in relationship (see Physical Abuse
chapter of this *Planner*).

10. Review the extended family
history in regard to divorce

impact personal and social life, immediate and extended family relationship, and spirituality. (14)

13. Each partner verbalize a dedication to being sensitive to their children's thoughts, needs, and feelings during this time of insecurity. (15, 16, 17)

14. Agree on how and what to tell the children regarding the impending divorce. Practice the disclosure. (18)

15. Report on the experience of telling the children regarding the divorce, and agree on what further explanation or support may be necessary. (18, 19)

16. Each partner identify how he/she has allowed own anger to get out of control, causing unnecessary pain to the other. Agree to the need for better control. (20, 21, 22, 23, 24)

17. Each partner exercises anger-control skills (e.g., identifying escalating level of anger, using time-out techniques, refocusing on problem at hand) to negotiate the future of the relationship and parenting without screaming, intimidating, or evoking fear. (22, 23, 24)

18. Agree to whether and when one partner will move out. Negotiate the terms and conditions of the separation. (25)

and have each partner verbalize how this history may be affecting the decision to divorce.

11. Ask each partner to identify his/her subcultural identification and its influence on attitude about divorce (e.g., ethnicity, religious identification). Facilitate a resolution of conflict between behavior and beliefs.

12. Ask each partner to turn to the other and express in what ways self has (a) contributed to the downfall of the relationship, and (b) in what ways he/she has attempted to make the relationship work.

13. Ask both partners to verbalize their points of view on (a) the pros and cons of preserving the relationship, and (b) the pros and cons of separation or divorce.

14. Ask each partner to verbalize the implications of divorce in the following areas: (a) personal, (b) family (including children), (c) religious, and (d) social. Have the other partner paraphrase the first person's statements in each area to increase understanding and empathy between the two partners.

15. Sensitize the partners to the upheaval that children face by having them discuss the anticipated effects on their children.

19. Clarify new boundaries by establishing the new goals of the altered relationship (e.g., to provide the children with healthy home environments), the new prescriptions (e.g., each person supporting the other's role in the children's lives), and proscriptions (e.g., no future sexual contact). (26)

20. Each partner constructively express his/her emotional pain about the decline of the relationship and verbalize new short- and long-term goals for personal life. (27)

21. Verbalize an understanding of the differences between litigation, arbitration, and mediation as means of dissolving the marriage. Agree to one choice. (28)

22. Develop a coparenting agreement that is in the best interest of the children and deals with the child's residence, emotional support, financial support, and custody and visitation. (29)

23. Each partner outline a plan for how to increase his/her social life and strengthen his/her social and spiritual support system. (30)

24. Cooperate with bringing children to sessions in order to listen to them express their emotional reactions and needs. (31)

25. Accept and follow through on referral to divorce and

16. Assign parents to read *How to Help Your Child Overcome Your Divorce* (Benedek and Brown, 1995), *The Parent's Book About Divorce* (Gardner, 1991) and/or *Mom's House, Dad's House* (Ricci, 1997).

17. Have partners verbally contract with each other and with the therapist that all decisions in the divorce and separation process will be made with the "best interests of the children" as the paramount concern.

18. Using role-playing techniques, have the partners rehearse telling the children together about the divorce. Have them explain that (*a*) they both love the children very much, (*b*) they plan to divorce, (*c*) the divorce is not the children's fault, (*d*) there is nothing the children can do to get parents back together, and (*e*) they will both continue to love and see the children.

19. Review the experience of parents telling the children of the divorce or separation and probe the needs for further explanation or support. Press for agreement on this issue.

20. Ask each partner to describe times when his/her own anger was destructive to the other partner.

single-parent support groups.

26. Verbalize the effect divorce has had on religious beliefs and practices. (33)

___. _____
_____
___. _____
_____
___. _____
_____

21. Clarify for the clients the role of the therapist: to (*a*) aid the family in making the separation or divorce transition, and (*b*) help both partners deal with the turbulent emotions experienced during this process. Emphasize that the therapist's role is to serve the best interests of all family members. However, he/she will not be a mediator or judge.

22. Teach partners to recognize the gradations of anger and to take steps to cool down (e.g., practice relaxation and deep-breathing exercises, take time out for 15 minutes, go for a walk) before self-control becomes eroded.

23. Ask each partner to identify hot topics and practice in-session cognitive rehearsal about how to cope with such topics adaptively.

24. Have both partners practice time out (agree to a pause in the conversation when anger begins to elevate) while discussing an emotional topic in session.

25. Facilitate a discussion and decision-making, pending legal advice, regarding whether and when one partner will move out of the house. If an in-house separation is financially necessary, negotiate the terms and conditions.

26. Facilitate an agreement between the partners about

what forms of contact are acceptable (e.g., planning around children's activities) and what are prohibited (e.g., sexual intimacies).

27. Using individual sessions as needed, allow each partner to express his/her anger, disappointment, and disapproval over what has happened. Balance these expressions of hurt with an elicitation of his/her goals for coping with short-term and long-term situations with the other partner and children.

28. Educate partners regarding the three choices available for dissolving the marriage: (*a*) litigation, which is an adversarial legal process; (*b*) arbitration, in which a third party, whom each partner typically helps choose, makes decisions regarding property and custody; and (c) mediation, in which the partners come to their own agreement, with the help of a trained mediator.

29. Facilitate the development of a coparenting agreement in which the partners pledge that (*a*) the children's primary residence will be established in their best interests; (*b*) neither parent will belittle the other and his/her family members in front of the children; (*c*) parents will avoid placing the children

in loyalty conflicts; and (*d*) the parents agree regarding terms of financial support for the children.

30. Using individual sessions, assist each partner in developing a varied social network (e.g., asking others to socialize; beginning or increasing involvement in club, community, volunteer, and/or church activities; dating).

31. Conduct parent-child sessions when necessary, to ensure that the children's emotional needs are being attended to.

32. Encourage partners to attend local divorce therapy groups and/or self-help groups (e.g., Parents without Partners).

33. Assess whether the divorce has affected either partner's religious and spiritual connections, and assist in problem-solving if he/she has difficulty reestablishing connections (e.g. switching parishes, investigating churches that welcome divorced members).

___. _____

_____

___. _____

_____

___. _____

_____

DIAGNOSTIC SUGGESTIONS

Axis I	309.0	Adjustment Disorder With Depressed Mood
	309.24	Adjustment Disorder With Anxiety
	309.28	Adjustment Disorder With Mixed Anxiety and Depressed Mood
	309.4	Adjustment Disorder With Mixed Disturbance of Emotions and Conduct
	305.00	Alcohol Abuse
	303.90	Alcohol Dependence
	300.4	Dysthymic Disorder
	300.02	Generalized Anxiety Disorder
	296.x	Major Depressive Disorder
	V61.1	Physical Abuse of Adult, 995.81 Victim
	V61.1	Partner Relational Problem
	_____	_____
	_____	_____
Axis II	301.6	Dependent Personality Disorder
	301.83	Borderline Personality Disorder
	301.81	Narcissistic Personality Disorder
	_____	_____
	_____	_____

SEXUAL ABUSE

BEHAVIORAL DEFINITIONS

1. Verbal demands for sexual interaction.
2. Physical pressure exerted to get partner to fulfill sexual demands.
3. Threat of force used to get partner to cooperate with demands for intercourse or other sexual activity.
4. Verbal demands for a type of sexual activity with which the partner is clearly uncomfortable.
5. Physical demands for a type of sexual activity with which the partner is clearly uncomfortable.
6. Criticism of partner for being "frigid" or "impotent."
7. Threats to withhold sex from partner in the future.
8. Threats to have sex with someone else.
9. Threats to leave partner.
10. Very low desire for sexual activity due to resentment or fear related to coercion used by partner for sexual activity.

Sexual abuse usually occurs in conjunction with psychological and physical abuse. In fact, sexual abuse with physical force is much less common than physical abuse. Thus, sexual abuse with physical force is a more unusual pattern in a relationship, and it is difficult to change. Psychological abuse, particularly in the form of threats and critical comments about the partner's sexual style, is much more common, and is an issue that all marital and family therapists should be prepared to address. The level of coercion and abused partner's degree of fear of the abusive partner should be assessed individually (i.e., without the abusive partner present). If either coercion and/or fear are high, then individual therapy with the abusive partner, usually the male, is in order before conjoint therapy. Once conjoint therapy begins, clinicians should make diagnostic judgements about the need for combinations of individual and conjoint therapy.

11. Avoidance of any sexual interaction due to resentment or fear relating to coercion used by partner for sexual activity.
12. Complaints by one or both partners about lack of love and caring.
13. Avoidance of communication with partner regarding sexual matters.

___. _____

_____

___. _____

_____

___. _____

_____

LONG-TERM GOALS

1. Eliminate all types of coercion (physical or verbal) used by one partner to get the other partner to fulfill sexual demands.
2. Eliminate critical comments of partner's sexual style.
3. Eliminate threats to have sex with others.
4. Eliminate threats to leave the relationship.
5. Increase general relationship satisfaction.
6. Increase communication in general and about sexual matters in particular.
7. Increase desire for and enjoyment of healthy, voluntary sexual activity.
8. Develop accepting attitude of variability in "normal" sexual activity.
9. Develop accepting attitude of changes in sexual activity across a life span.
10. Evaluate alternatives to current relationship.

___. _____

_____

___. _____

_____

___. _____

_____

SHORT-TERM OBJECTIVES

1. Agree to a clear ground rule that no physical force will be employed for any sexual interaction. (1, 2)

2. Agree to a clear ground rule that sexual interactions will only be engaged in if both partners desire to engage in such activity. (3)

3. Verbalize an understanding of the fragility of sexual behavior and how it can become less functional with negative feedback or punishment. (4, 5)

4. Agree to a clear ground rule that there will be no threats to have sex with someone else. (6, 7)

5. Agree to a clear ground rule that there will be no threats to leave partner during the therapy process. (8)

6. Agree to a clear ground rule that there will be no physical aggression against the partner for any reason. (9, 10)

7. Describe the nature and extent of any psychological coercion used within the relationship. (11)

8. Describe the nature and extent of any physical aggression within the relationship. (12)

9. State the degree of fear that has resulted from coercion within the relationship, and

THERAPEUTIC INTERVENTIONS

1. Obtain verbal commitment from partners not to employ physical force for any sexual interaction.

2. Obtain written commitment from partners not to employ physical force for any sexual interaction.

3. Educate clients that to have a positive sexual relationship, the sexual activity must be acceptable to both partners.

4. Educate clients that pressure to have sexual activity usually leads to sexual aversions and/or avoidance and dislike of the partner.

5. Educate clients that sexual behavior is one of the most susceptible of all human behaviors to aversive control, and that aversive control of sexual activity can quickly lead to lack of interest and sexual dysfunction of the partner.

6. Obtain verbal commitment from partners not to threaten to have sex with someone else.

7. Obtain commitment from both partners not to have sex with someone else during the course of therapy. This commitment should be obtained individually (i.e., not in the presence of the other partner).

what effect the fear has had on loving feelings, sexual arousal, and sexual desire. (13)

10. Verbalize an understanding of the effects on a relationship of control and misuse of power in American society. (14, 15, 16)

11. Describe the history of the sexual relationship and identify where conflicts about sexual matters began to occur. (17, 18)

12. Verbalize an understanding of the norms of sexual activity and how patterns within the relationship relate to those norms. (19)

13. Describe the positive aspects of the nonsexual portion of the relationship. (20)

14. Describe the positive aspects of the sexual portion of the relationship. (21)

15. Communicate openly and without criticism, especially about sexual matters. (22, 23, 24)

16. Describe the causes for the decline in frequency and enjoyment of sexual encounters. (25)

17. Abusive partner describe any physical abuse of self or others in childhood and how these experiences could affect current abuse of partner. (26)

18. Abused partner describe any physical abuse of self or

8. Obtain verbal commitment from partners not to threaten to leave the relationship during therapy. (An agreement about a particular time span for the therapy should be developed at the beginning of treatment.)

9. Obtain verbal commitment from partners not to employ physical force against the other partner for any reason.

10. Obtain written commitment from partners not to employ physical force against the other partner for any reason.

11. Ask both partners to describe the extent to which psychological coercion is used in the relationship in general.

12. Ask both partners to describe the extent to which physical aggression is used in the relationship in general.

13. Ask both partners to describe any fears they have of their partners and how this fear affects the intimate aspects of the relationship.

14. Discuss the role of patriarchy in American society.

15. Discuss how the controlling partner misuses his/her power.

16. Educate clients regarding how controlling behaviors lead to dislike and avoidance of partner.

17. Have clients describe their initial expectations about their sexual life.

others in childhood and how these experiences could affect his/her toleration of current sexual abuse. (27)

19. Abusive partner describe developmental history of hostile feelings toward the opposite sex that affect current disrespectful treatment of partner. (28)

20. Abusive partner verbalize feelings of low self-esteem and lack of trust in others that feeds the abusive behavior toward partner. (29)

21. Verbalize understanding that sexual coercion or degrading criticism changes sexual behaviors into acts of domination and/or submission. (30)

22. Describe any traumatic sexual experiences experienced outside of the relationship. (31)

23. Agree to terminate any sexual activity that triggers negative emotions related to earlier sexual trauma. (32)

24. Engage in sensate focus with partner. (33)

25. Discuss sensate focus activities with partner in therapy sessions, and change sexual stimulation activities based on feedback from partner. (34)

26. Assess alternatives to relationship, and receive refer-

18. Have clients describe how their expectations about their sexual life changed with the beginning of conflict over intimacy.

19. Assist clients in interpreting how the frequency, nature, and satisfaction of their sexual encounters corresponds to that of others of their age in our culture.

20. Ask partners to describe the positive, nonsexual aspects of their current relationship.

21. Ask partners to describe the positive, sexual aspects of their current relationship.

22. Have each partner listen without interrupting while the other partner speaks about a nonsexual matter, and then have him/her validate without interpretation what the other said.

23. Have each partner communicate about a sexual matter without interruption, and then obtain validation from the other partner.

24. Provide feedback and interpretation to partners about their communication styles.

25. Ask partners to describe the perceived causes for decline in frequency and enjoyment of sexual activity.

26. Explore with abusive or critical partner whether there has been a history of physical abuse of self or others in childhood family experience.

rals for safely escaping from abuse. (35, 36, 37)

__. _____
    _____
__. _____
    _____
__. _____
    _____

27. Explore with abused partner whether there is a history of physical abuse of self or others in childhood family experience that could be a basis for expecting or tolerating abuse now.

28. Explore with abusive partner whether there is a history of anger toward the opposite sex that has roots in unresolved childhood experiences.

29. Probe the degree to which abuser trusts that sexual activity would be freely and happily engaged in by the other partner if coercion was not present. (That is, does he/she feel lovable and able to trust anyone?)

30. Confront sexual coercion or belittling criticism as a means of domination that degrades the other partner from role as lover to that of victim.

31. Have each client identify any traumatic sexual experiences that he/she encountered with anyone.

32. Advise partners to cease any sexual activity that triggers memories of traumatic events.

33. Instruct each client in use of sensate focus technique to teach partner how to touch self.

34. Obtain feedback from clients about the sensate focus exercises, and assist in minimizing any behav-

iors that affect either partner negatively.

35. In an individual session, discuss with sexually abused client the alternatives to the current relationship.

36. In a confidential individual session, help sexually abused client evaluate the alternatives to the current relationship.

37. If necessary, refer sexually abused client to an agency for battered women and/or to a shelter.

___. _____
     _____
___. _____
     _____
___. _____
     _____

DIAGNOSTIC SUGGESTIONS

Axis I:	302.72	Female Sexual Arousal Disorder
	302.73	Female Orgasmic Disorder
	302.71	Hypoactive Sexual Desire Disorder
	312.34	Intermittent Explosive Disorder
	302.74	Male Orgasmic Disorder
	302.9	Sexual Disorder NOS
	V61.1	Sexual Abuse of Partner, 995.81 Victim
	302.79	Sexual Aversion Disorder
	V61.1	Physical Abuse of Partner, 995.81 Victim
	_____	_____
	_____	_____
Axis II:	301.7	Antisocial Personality Disorder
	_____	_____
	_____	_____

SEXUAL DYSFUNCTION

BEHAVIORAL DEFINITIONS

1. Consistently very low desire for—or no pleasurable anticipation of—sexual activity.
2. Strong avoidance of—and/or repulsion to—any and all sexual contact in spite of a relationship of mutual caring and respect.
3. Recurrent lack of usual physiological response of sexual excitement and arousal (e.g., erection, vaginal lubrication).
4. Consistent lack of subjective sense of enjoyment and pleasure during sexual activity.
5. Persistent delay in—or absence of—reaching orgasm after achieving arousal, in spite of sensitive sexual pleasuring by a caring partner.
6. Genital pain before, during, or after sexual intercourse.
7. Consistent or recurring involuntary spasm of the vagina (i.e., vaginismus) that prohibits penetration for sexual intercourse.
8. Expressions of general relationship dissatisfaction.
9. Verbalizations of a lack of love and/or caring by one or both partners.
10. Avoidance of communication regarding sexual matters.
11. Critical comments regarding the partner's lack of sexual responsiveness.
12. Statements of low self-esteem by partner with sexual dysfunction.
13. Statements of low self-esteem by partner who perceives the sexual dysfunction of other partner to be his/her fault.
14. Depressed mood in one or both partners.

—. _____
  _____
—. _____
  _____

—. _____

_____

LONG-TERM GOALS

1. Increase desire for and enjoyment of sexual activity.
2. Increase physiological arousal during sexual interactions.
3. Maintain physiological arousal during sexual interactions.
4. Reach orgasm on a regular basis.
5. Eliminate pain associated with any aspect of the sexual interaction. Eliminate spasms that prevent intromission.
6. Increase communication in general, and particularly about sexual matters.
7. Increase general relationship satisfaction.
8. Reduce depressive symptomatology.
9. Increase both partners' self-esteem.
10. Develop accepting attitude toward variability in "normal" sexual activity.
11. Develop accepting attitudes toward changes in the intensity and frequency of sexual activity across a life span.

—. _____

_____

—. _____

_____

—. _____

_____

SHORT-TERM OBJECTIVES	THERAPEUTIC INTERVENTIONS
1. Describe the history of the sexual relationship and identify where conflicts about sexual matters began to occur. (1, 2, 3)	1. Assess the frequency of sexual interactions across the history of the relationship.
2. Identify the positive aspects of the nonsexual portion of the relationship. (4, 5)	2. Assess the partners' enjoyment of sexual interactions across history of the relationship.

3. Describe the positive aspects of the sexual relationship. (6, 7)

4. Communicate openly and without criticism, especially about sexual matters. (8, 9, 10)

5. Identify sexual expectations in the relationship and how they have changed across time. (11, 12, 13)

6. Describe any past traumatic experience that now may be impacting on the sexual interaction. (14, 15)

7. Identify any religious beliefs or training that may be interfering with experiencing pleasure from sexual activity. (16)

8. Cease any activity that triggers memories of past traumatic experiences until the feelings related to that activity can be resolved. (17)

9. Discuss the development of sexual attitudes in family of origin, identifying those experiences which enhance and those that deter one or both partners from currently experiencing sexual pleasure. (18)

10. Verbalize an emotional detachment from early family experiences regarding sexuality that has deterred partners from current experience of pleasure. (19)

11. Identify and resolve, if possible, any physical disorder

3. Ask partners to describe the perceived causes of decline in sexual activity and enjoyment thereof.

4. Ask partners to describe the positive nonsexual aspects of the beginning of their relationship.

5. Ask partners to describe the positive nonsexual aspects of their current relationship.

6. Ask partners to describe the positive sexual aspects of the beginning of their relationship.

7. Ask partners to describe the positive sexual aspects of their current relationship.

8. Ask partners to communicate with each other about a nonsexual matter. Listener should allow partner to speak without interruption and, to demonstrate understanding, should paraphrase speaker's intent.

9. Ask clients to communicate with each other about a sexual matter. Listener should allow partner to speak without interruption and, to demonstrate understanding, should paraphrase speaker's intent.

10. Provide feedback and interpretation to partners about their communication styles.

11. Ask each client to describe initial expectations about his/her sexual life.

12. Have each client describe how expectations about

or medication that is inhibiting sexual desire. (20, 21)

12. Verbalize feelings regarding body image and how it relates to sexual functioning. (22)

13. Verbalize an improved body image due to increased exercise, improved dress, and/or more healthy diet. (23, 24)

14. Identify causes for and remedies to low self-esteem within the relationship. (25)

15. Identify whether a perceived or real emotionally intimate or sexual relationship with another partner creates continuing resentment and/or jealousy. (26)

16. Verbalize whether any homosexual activity and/or fantasy impedes sexual functioning with partner, openly acknowledging plans for future direction of sexual interest. (27, 28)

17. Report an increase in sexual thoughts and/or fantasy when not engaged in sexual activity with partner. (29, 30, 31)

18. Read books and/or watch educational videos on sexual functioning and sexuality. (31, 32)

19. Engage in sensate focus activity alone and with partner. (33)

18. Discuss sensate focus activities with partner in therapy

his/her sexual life have changed.

13. Assist clients in interpreting how the frequency and satisfaction of their sexual encounters correspond to that of others of their ages.

14. Have each client discuss any past traumatic sexual experiences.

15. Probe about thoughts during sexual activities and ascertain whether the traumatic sexual encounter triggers negative emotions during sexual overtures or activity. If found, resolve past traumas that impact current sexual pleasure.

16. Examine whether religious beliefs or training interferes with engaging in sexual activity desired by either partner. If interferences exist, attempt to neutralize current impact, or define acceptable sexual practice.

17. Recommend that partners temporarily cease any sexual activity that triggers memories of traumatic events, until traumatic memories are properly resolved.

18. Assist partners in identifying family-of-origin experiences that influence current positive and negative sexual experiences.

19. Explore feelings related to early family experiences that have a negative impact

sessions, and change sexual
stimulation activities based
on feedback from partner.
(34)

—. _____
   _____
—. _____
   _____
—. _____
   _____

on current sexual experi-
ence. Encourage a differentiation between the past
and the here-and-now.

20. Assess role of any known or
possible existing physical
condition that could interfere with sexual functioning
(e.g., diabetes, substance
abuse, depression, anxiety
disorders).

21. Assess role of any medication that could interfere
with sexual functioning
(e.g., antihypertensive medication, antidepressant
medication).

22. Explore whether the
decrease in the frequency
and range of sexual activities is related to a decline in
body image (e.g., increased
body weight, lack of muscle
tone, or the residual effects
of surgery).

23. Encourage a positive
change in attitude regarding client's body image.

24. Assign a change in exercise,
dress, and/or diet to enhance
client's body image.

25. Assess the role of self-
esteem in sexual functioning, and identify the factors
in the relationship that lead
to positive and negative
feelings.

26. Probe feelings that relate to
perceived or actual extramarital affairs, and make
certain that such relationships have stopped.

27. Assess (in individual session) whether there are homosexual thoughts or activities that interfere with heterosexual functioning.

28. If there are homosexual activities or fantasies that interfere with the couple's sexual relationship, explore the sexual identity issue and its implication for the future of heterosexual relationships.

29. Request that clients indulge in sexual fantasies that increase sexual desire toward partner.

30. Request that clients read material on sexual fantasies. Examples might include *My Secret Garden* (Friday, 1995), *Women on Top* (Friday, 1993), *Becoming Orgasmic: A Sexual Growth Program for Women* (Heiman and LoPiccolo, 1988).

31. If religious views permit, clients, especially females, can be encouraged to purchase educational videos of sexual activities to teach enhancement of fantasy, masturbation, and a variety of heterosexual sexual behaviors. Examples include *Self-Loving* (Dodson), and *Better Sex Video Series: Vols. 1–3* (Sinclair Institute). (See References for Videos in Bibliography.)

32. Suggest that clients read books on sexual behavior and sexual functioning, such as *Sex for Dummies*

(Westheimer, 1995), *The New Male Sexuality* (Zilbergeld, 1992), *The New Joy of Sex* (Comfort, 1991), *The Gift of Sex* (Penner and Penner, 1981), and *When a Woman's Body Says No to Sex* (Valins, 1992).

33. Instruct clients in use of sensate focus to learn how to touch each other.

34. Obtain feedback from clients about the sensate focus exercises, and assist in minimizing any behaviors that affect either partner negatively.

—. _____
_____

—. _____
_____

—. _____
_____

DIAGNOSTIC SUGGESTIONS

Axis I	302.73	Female Orgasmic Disorder
	302.72	Female Sexual Arousal Disorder
	625.8	Female Hypoactive Sexual Desire Disorder Due to Axis III Disorder
	302.71	Hypoactive Sexual Desire Disorder
	302.72	Male Erectile Disorder
	302.74	Male Orgasmic Disorder
	607.84	Male Hypoactive Sexual Desire Disorder Due to Axis III Disorder
	302.75	Premature Ejaculation
	V61.21	Sexual Abuse of Child, 995.3 Victim
	302.79	Sexual Aversion Disorder
	302.9	Sexual Disorder NOS
	_____	_____
	_____	_____

WORK/HOME ROLE STRAIN

BEHAVIORAL DEFINITIONS

1. Perception by one partner that self or family is not placed as a high enough priority in the other partner's life because of too great emphasis on employment interests.
2. Contention by one or both partners that the other partner is not meeting his/her fair share of responsibilities in relationship, family, home maintenance, or work.
3. Partner conflict over current allocation of time to work, home, and chore roles.
4. Arguments between partners over role imbalances.
5. Perceived difficulty in meeting role expectations.
6. Perceived disorganization or time inefficiencies in attempts to meet key role responsibilities.

__. _____
_____
__. _____
_____
__. _____
_____

LONG-TERM GOALS

1. Meet the basic responsibilities of work, relationship, and family in a mutually agreeable manner.
2. Satisfactorily balance the competing demands of work and family.
3. Clarify the values that guide life choices and time allocation.

4. Bring time allocation into harmony with espoused values.
5. Develop tolerance and empathy for the other partner's attempts to meet conflicting role demands.
6. Change thinking and behavioral patterns that create conflict or interfere with sincere attempts to meet conflicting role demands.

__. _____
    _____
    _____
__. _____
    _____
    _____
__. _____
    _____

SHORT-TERM OBJECTIVES

1. Verbally define current level of satisfaction and stress in work and family roles. (1, 2, 3)
2. Verbally identify how current work, relationship, and home roles are met. (4, 5, 6, 7)
3. Identify how the demands of employment interfere with the responsibilities of home and family, and identify how the demands of family or relationship interfere with work responsibilities. (8, 9)
4. Identify how work stress leads to relationship conflicts. (10)
5. Specify the conflicting expectations of work versus home. (11)
6. Clarify, write, and discuss personal guidelines or val-

THERAPEUTIC INTERVENTIONS

1. Assess each partner's satisfaction with work and family roles.
2. Probe the level of stress due to work/home role strain experienced by either partner.
3. Query both partners about their work schedules (e.g., How many hours do they typically work? What shift does each work? Do they bring work home?).
4. Ask the couple to describe a typical workday and a typical weekend day (e.g., What time do they get up? What is their morning routine? How does the workday go? What is their evening routine? Do they have set patterns, or is there a lot of variability each day?).
5. Have the couple describe how the current role

ues that are expected to influence important life role enactment. (12, 13)

7. Identify how espoused values conflict with actual decisions regarding allocation of time and other resources. (14)

8. Identify how parents, friends, religious beliefs, culture, and subculture have influenced expectations regarding own and partner's roles in the relationship. (15)

9. Verbalize an understanding of the other partner's dilemma in meeting competing role demands. (16, 17)

10. Verbalize an understanding of the other partner's feelings generated by the current role arrangement. (18, 19)

11. List the negative self-talk conclusions that accompany negative emotions over the current role arrangements. (20, 21)

12. Identify whether the thoughts or conclusions promote problem resolution, are directly relevant to the situation, and are accurate. (22)

13. Verbalize self-talk conclusions that promote problem resolution, are directly related to the situation, and are reality-based. (23)

14. State conclusion desired regarding partner's role

arrangement came about. Did they discuss their current family/work time and responsibility allocations explicitly, or did the current arrangement evolve implicitly?

6. Assess how chores at home are divided between family members (e.g., Is there an explicit plan?).

7. If the couple has children, assess each partner's satisfaction with the other's involvement in caring for the children.

8. Ask the couple to describe the ways that family demands interfere with the employment role.

9. Ask the couple to describe the ways that employment demands interfere with the family role.

10. Ask the couple to describe the ways in which work stress may precipitate relationship conflicts.

11. Ask each partner to write down, in two columns, the behaviors that are expected of them at work and at home. Ask them to read theirs out loud and discuss any incompatible expectations.

12. Assign reading of *Seven Habits of Highly Effective Families* (Covey, 1997).

13. For homework, ask partners to write their personal mission statement that reflects

behavior and identify what self could do to increase the probability of the behavior occurring. (24, 25)

15. Identify and list the activities that must be performed at work and home. (26)

16. Prioritize the activities of home and work and then mutually agree to a time allocation for each partner to each task. (27)

17. Identify areas of disagreement regarding time allocation, and attempt to reach mutually agreeable solutions. (28, 29, 30, 31)

18. Enact and evaluate solutions to time-allocation problems. (32, 33)

19. Contract with partner regarding both partners' ongoing role expectations, and how recurrent problematic situations will be resolved. (34, 35)

20. Cope with limited time resources by identifying and contracting to meet basic family or relationship needs. (36, 37)

__. _____
_____
__. _____
_____
__. _____
_____

their personally held values and bring it to session.

14. Ask partners to read their mission statement, and ask if they are carrying it out (e.g., if the mission statement includes making both home and work high priorities, does the time allocation/quality reflect this?).

15. Have both partners describe what expectations they perceive parents, friends, subcultural groups, and society have for them in their work and home roles.

16. Ask partners to define for each other the dilemmas they face in trying to meet their varied and sometimes competing role demands.

17. While one partner serves as speaker, have the other use positive listener skills (i.e., paraphrasing and reflecting) to demonstrate that he/she is trying to understand and empathize with the speaker's dilemmas.

18. Ask each partner to describe how both the positive and negative aspects of the current role arrangement affect him/her emotionally. For example, "I feel proud and successful about my work accomplishments lately, but I feel that I'm missing a lot of what's going on with the kids."

19. While one partner serves as speaker, have the listener

validate and empathize with his/her perspective regarding the gains and losses of the current role arrangement.

20. Assign partners to write as homework the thoughts or self-talk conclusions associated with negative feelings over the current role arrangement.

21. Ask each partner to read his/her thought-tracking homework in session.

22. Assess with partners whether each thought or conclusion (*a*) would be helpful in getting the desired outcome if it was verbalized; (*b*) is directly related to the specific situation described (i.e., is situationally-specific, not global); and (c) is accurate (i.e., actual evidence can be cited to support the conclusion).

23. If any thought or conclusion fails to meet all three criteria, have client rework the thought or conclusion so that it does meet all three criteria. For example, "He doesn't care about his children," can become "He seems to be having a hard time finding time for both work and home lately. After the kids are in bed, I'll ask him if he feels up to discussing the strain."

24. For each thought or conclusion identified, have client state what he/she would

like the other partner to do instead of stating what the other partner is doing.

25. Have each partner identify what he/she can do to increase the probability of attaining desired behavior from the other partner, versus complaining about the other's behavioral faults. For example, "She doesn't spend enough time at home," can become "I want to be supportive so that our home is one she would want to come home to."

26. Ask each partner to identify and list the current activities that must be performed at home and work.

27. Have partners prioritize the key short-term and long-term goals in their work, family, and chore roles. Assign each partner to allocate his/her weekly work, family, and chore time based on the identified priorities.

28. If either partner is upset with the proposed allocation of time, have him/her use pinpointing skills to identify the problem. For example, "It upsets me when I see that your time allocation places most of the daily burden for child care on me. I'd like to have more help." Have other partner use paraphrasing and/or reflection to indicate understanding.

29. Ask partners to brainstorm possible sources of assis-

tance to ease home and work role demands (e.g., family members, child care, household help, project delegation).

30. Ask partners to brainstorm ways of reallocating their time to provide mutual support and benefits.

31. Assist partners in evaluating the pros and cons of the brainstormed solutions and help them choose a mutually preferred solution.

32. Have partners (a) agree exactly how the solution would be carried out, (b) contract with each other to enact it, and (c) write down their perceptions of the results (for discussion in a future session).

33. Discuss partners' perceptions of the results and help them determine whether the solution could be improved in any way.

34. Ask partners to write and sign a work/home contract that details explicit expectations, requirements, and rewards for each partner in carrying out his/her responsibilities.

35. Have partners discuss and develop explicit written agreements regarding difficult daily work/home strains (e.g., Bill will watch the baby for 15 minutes while Beth changes out of her work clothes).

36. If partners' resources are insufficient to meet current standards, help partners identify whether standards can be explicitly modified to meet resources (e.g., partners will clean for company and to maintain adequate levels of hygiene, but otherwise will clean the house no more than once per month).

37. If work schedules make family time difficult to schedule, help partners establish brief routines that maintain some family contact and closeness (e.g., a short evening phone ritual during the working partner's break).

___. _____

_____

___. _____

_____

___. _____

_____

DIAGNOSIS SUGGESTIONS

Axis I:	309.24	Adjustment Disorder With Anxiety
	309.0	Adjustment Disorder With Depressed Mood
	309.28	Adjustment Disorder With Mixed Anxiety and Depressed Mood
	300.4	Dysthymic Disorder
	300.02	Generalized Anxiety Disorder
	296.x	Major Depressive Episode
	_____	_____
	_____	_____

Appendix A

BIBLIOTHERAPY SUGGESTIONS

Alcohol Abuse

Johnson, V. (1980). *I'll quit tomorrow*. New York: Harper and Row.

Miller, W. R., & Muñoz, R. F. (1982). *How to control your drinking* (Rev. ed.). Albuquerque, NM: University of New Mexico Press.

National Institute on Alcohol Abuse and Alcoholism. (1996). *How to cut down on your drinking* (NIH pamphlet No. 96-3770). Available from NIAAA, PO Box 10686, Rockville, MD 20849-0686. (301) 443-3860. Web site: http://www.niaaa.nih.gov.

National Institute on Alcohol Abuse and Alcoholism. (1996). *Alcoholism: Getting the facts* (NIH Publication No. 96-4153). Available from NIAAA, PO Box 10686, Rockville, MD 20849-0686. (301) 443-3860. Web site: http://www.niaaa.nih.gov.

Anger

Rosellini, G., & Worden, M. (1986). *Of course you're angry*. San Francisco: Harper Hazelden.

Rubin, T. I. (1969). The *angry book*. New York: MacMillan.

Tavris, C. (1989). *Anger: The misunderstood emotion*. New York: Touchstone.

Anxiety

Barlow, D. H., & Craske, M. (1994). *Mastering your anxiety and panic—Patient's workbook*. San Antonio, TX: The Psychological Corporation.

Craske, M., & Barlow, D. (1992) *Mastering Your Anxiety and Worry—Patient's workbook*. San Antonio, TX: The Psychological Corporation.

Blended-Family Problems

Kaufman, T. S. (1993). *The combined family: A guide to creating successful step-relationships*. New York: Plenum.

Communication

Beck, A. T. (1988). *Love is never enough*. New York: Harper and Row.
Fincham, F. D., Fernandes, L. O. L., & Humphreys, L. (1993). *Communicating in relationships: A guide for couples and professionals*. Champaign, IL: Research Press.
Gottman, J. M. (1995). *Why marriages succeed or fail*. New York: Fireside.
Markman, H., Stanley, S., & Blumberg, S. L. (1994). *Fighting for your marriage*. San Francisco: Jossey-Bass. A companion videotape series is available from (800) 366-0166.
Notarius, C., & Markman, H. (1993). *We can work it out*. New York: Putnam.
Tannen, D. (1990). *You just don't understand*. New York: Ballantine.

Dependency

Beattie, M. (1987). *Co-dependent no more*. San Francisco: Harper.

Depression Independent of Relationship Problems

Burns, D. D. (1980). *Feeling good: The new mood therapy*. New York: Signet.
Golant, M., & Golant, S. K. (1997). *What to do when someone you love is depressed: A self-help and help others guide*. New York: Villard.
Lewinsohn, P. M., Muñoz, R. F., Youngren, M. A., & Zeiss, A. M. (1992). *Control your depression*. New York: Fireside.
Rosen, L. E., & Amador, X. F. (1996). *When someone you love is depressed: How to help your loved one without losing yourself.* New York: Fireside.

Depression Due to Relationship Problems

Burns, D. D. (1980). *Feeling good: The new mood therapy*. New York: Signet.

Disillusionment With Relationship

Covey, Stephen. (1997). *The seven habits of highly effective families: Building a beautiful family culture in a turbulent world*. New York: Golden Books.
O'Hanlon, B., & Hudson, P. (1995). *Love is a verb*. New York: Norton.

Eating Disorder

National Institute of Mental Health. (1994). *Eating Disorders.* (Brochure No. 94-3477). Available from NIMH Public Inquiries, 5600 Fishers Lane, Room 7C-02, MSC 8030, Bethesda, MD 20892-8030. Web site: http://www.nimh.nih.gov/publist/puborder.htm.

Infidelity

Pittman, F. (1990). *Private lies: Infidelity and betrayal of intimacy.* New York: Norton.
Spring. J. A. (1996). *After the affair: Healing the pain and rebuilding trust when a partner has been unfaithful.* New York: HarperCollins.

Jealousy

Kushner, H. S. (1997). *How good do we have to be?* New York: Little, Brown.

Job Stress

Covey, S. R., Merrill, A. R., & Merrill, R. R. (1996). *First things first.* New York: Fireside.

One Partner Unwilling to Attend Therapy

Beck, A. T. (1988). *Love is never enough.* New York: Harper and Row.
Covey, Stephen. (1997). *The seven habits of highly effective families.* New York: Golden Books.
Kramer, P. D. (1997). *Should you leave?* New York: Scribner.

Parenting Conflicts—Adolescents

Forgatch, M., & Patterson, G. R. (1987). *Parents and adolescents: Vol II: Family problem solving.* Eugene, OR: Castalia.
Patterson, G. R., & Forgatch, M. (1987). *Parents and adolescents: Living together. Vol I: The basics.* Eugene, OR: Castalia.

Parenting Conflicts—Children

Patterson, G. R. (1975). *Families: Applications of social learning to family life.* Champaign, IL: Research Press.

Sanders, M. R. (1992). *Every parent: A positive approach to children's behavior.* Sydney: Addison-Wesley.

Sanders, M. R., Lynch, M. E., & Markie-Dadds, C. (1994). *Every parent's workbook: A positive guide to positive parenting.* Brisbane: Australia Academic Press.

Physical Abuse

Betancourt, M. & McAfee, R. E. (1997). *What to do when love turns violent: A practical resource for women in abusive relationships.* New York: Harper Perennial Library.

Jacobson, N.S., & Gottman, J. M. (1998). *When men batter women: New insights into ending abusive relationships.* New York: Simon and Schuster.

Murphy-Milano, S. (1996). *Defending our lives: Getting away from domestic violence and staying safe.* New York: Anchor Books.

Psychological Abuse

Evans, P. (1996). *The verbally abusive relationship: How to recognize it and how to respond.* Holbrook, MA: Adams.

Separation and Divorce

Benedek, E. P., & Brown, C. F. (1995). *How to help your child overcome your divorce.* Washington, DC: American Psychiatric Press.

Gardner, R. A. (1985). *The boys and girls book about divorce, with an introduction for parents.* New York: Bantam Books.

Gardner, R. A. (1991). *The parent's book about divorce.* New York: Bantam Books.

Krementz, J. (1984). *How it feels when parents divorce.* New York: Knopf.

Ricci, I. (1997). *Mom's house, dad's house: A complete guide for parents who are separated, divorced, or remarried.* New York: Fireside.

Sexual Abuse

Russell, D. E. H. (1990). *Rape in marriage.* Bloomington, IN: Indiana University Press.

Sexual Dysfunction

Comfort A. (1991). *The new joy of sex.* New York: Crown.

Friday, N. (1995). *My secret garden.* New York: Crown.

Friday, N. (1993). *Women on top: How real life has changed women's sexual fantasies.* New York: Pocket.

Heiman, J., & LoPiccolo, J. (1988). *Becoming orgasmic: A sexual growth program for women.* New York: Prentice-Hall. A companion videotape is available from Sinclair Institute, P.O. Box 8865, Chapel Hill, NC 27515. (800) 955-0888, Ext. 8NET2. Web site: http://www.bettersex.com.

Penner, C., & Penner, C. (1981). *The gift of sex.* Waco, TX: Word.

Valins, L. (1992). *When a woman's body says no to sex: Understanding and overcoming vaginismus.* New York: Penguin.

Westheimer, R. (1995). *Sex for dummies.* New York: IDG Books.

Zilbergeld, B. (1992). *The new male sexuality.* New York: Bantam.

Work/Home Role Strain

Covey, Stephen. (1997). *The seven habits of highly effective families: Building a beautiful family culture in a turbulent world.* New York: Golden Books.

Appendix B

INDEX OF DSM-IV CODES ASSOCIATED WITH PRESENTING PROBLEMS

Adjustment Disorder With Anxiety
309.24

Anxiety
Blame
Communication
Financial Conflict
Infidelity
Interventions with One Partner
Intolerance
Jealousy
Job Stress
Life-Changing Events
Loss of Love/Affection
Midlife Crisis
Parenting Conflicts—Adolescents
Parenting Conflicts—Children
Personality Differences
Physical Abuse
Recreational Activities Dispute
Separation and Divorce
Work/Home Role Strain

Adjustment Disorder With Depressed Mood
309.0

Anger
Blame
Communication
Depression Independent of Relationship Problems
Depression Due to Relationship Problems
Disillusionment with Relationship

Financial Conflict
Infidelity
Interventions with One Partner
Intolerance
Jealousy
Job Stress
Life-Changing Events
Loss of Love/Affection
Midlife Crisis
Parenting Conflicts—Adolescents
Parenting Conflicts—Children
Personality Differences
Physical Abuse
Psychological Abuse
Recreational Activities Dispute
Separation and Divorce
Work/Home Role Strain

Adjustment Disorders With Disturbance of Conduct
309.3

Anger
Blame
Communication
Interventions with One Partner
Intolerance
Jealousy
Parenting Conflicts—Adolescents
Parenting Conflicts—Children
Personality Differences
Physical Abuse
Psychological Abuse

Adjustment Disorder With Mixed Anxiety and Depressed Mood 309.28
  Anxiety
  Blame
  Communication
  Financial Conflict
  Infidelity
  Interventions with One Partner
  Intolerance
  Jealousy
  Job Stress
  Life-Changing Events
  Loss of Love/Affection
  Midlife Crisis
  Parenting Conflicts—Adolescents
  Parenting Conflicts—Children
  Personality Differences
  Physical Abuse
  Recreational Activities Dispute
  Separation and Divorce
  Work/Home Role Strain

Adjustment Disorder With Mixed Disturbance of Emotions and Conduct   309.4
  Blame
  Communication
  Intolerance
  Jealousy
  Parenting Conflicts—Adolescents
  Parenting Conflicts—Children
  Personality Differences
  Physical Abuse
  Separation and Divorce

Alcohol Abuse   305.00
  Alcohol Abuse
  Anger
  Blame
  Communication
  Disillusionment with Relationship
  Eating Disorder
  Financial Conflict
  Interventions with One Partner
  Intolerance
  Jealousy
  Life-Changing Events
  Physical Abuse
  Psychological Abuse
  Recreational Activities Dispute
  Separation and Divorce

Alcohol Dependence   303.90
  Alcohol Abuse
  Anger
  Blame
  Communication
  Disillusionment with Relationship
  Eating Disorder
  Financial Conflict
  Interventions with One Partner
  Intolerance
  Jealousy
  Life-Changing Events
  Physical Abuse
  Psychological Abuse
  Recreational Activities Dispute
  Separation and Divorce

Anorexia Nervosa   307.1
  Eating Disorder

Antisocial Personality Disorder 301.7
  Anger
  Blame
  Communication
  Financial Conflict
  Infidelity
  Interventions with One Partner
  Intolerance
  Jealousy
  Personality Differences
  Physical Abuse
  Psychological Abuse
  Sexual Abuse

Anxiety Disorder Due to Axis III Disorder   293.89
  Anxiety

Anxiety Disorder NOS   300.00
  Anxiety

Avoidant Personality Disorder   301.82
  Alcohol Abuse
  Dependency
  Job Stress

Bereavement   V62.82
  Depression Independent of Relationship Problems

Depression Due to Relationship
Problems

Bipolar I Disorder   296.xx
Anger
Communication
Infidelity
Interventions with One Partner
Jealousy

**Bipolar I Disorder, Single Manic
Episode**   296.0x
Financial Conflict

Borderline Personality Disorder
                                     301.83
Anger
Blame
Communication
Depression Independent of
Relationship Problems
Depression Due to Relationship
Problems
Eating Disorder
Interventions with One Partner
Intolerance
Jealousy
Loss of Love/Affection
Personality Differences
Physical Abuse
Psychological Abuse
Separation and Divorce

Bulimia Nervosa   307.51
Eating Disorder
Financial Conflict

Cannabis Dependence   304.30
Financial Conflict

Cyclothymic Disorder   301.13
Infidelity

Dependent Personality Disorder
                                     301.6
Alcohol Abuse
Dependency
Eating Disorder
Financial Conflict
Infidelity
Interventions with One Partner
Intolerance

Job Stress
Personality Differences
Physical Abuse
Psychological Abuse
Separation and Divorce

Depressive Disorder NOS   311
Dependency

Dysthymic Disorder   300.4
Alcohol Abuse
Communication
Dependency
Depression Independent of
Relationship Problems
Depression Due to Relationship
Problems
Disillusionment with Relationship
Interventions with One Partner
Intolerance
Jealousy
Job Stress
Life-Changing Events
Midlife Crisis
Physical Abuse
Psychological Abuse
Recreational Activities Dispute
Separation and Divorce
Work/Home Role Strain

Eating Disorder NOS   307.50
Eating Disorder

**Female Hypoactive Sexual Desire
Disorder Due to Axis III Disorder**
                                     625.8
Sexual Dysfunction

Female Orgasmic Disorder   302.73
Sexual Abuse
Sexual Dysfunction

Female Sexual Arousal Disorder
                                     302.72
Sexual Abuse
Sexual Dysfunction

Generalized Anxiety Disorder
                                     300.02
Anxiety
Job Stress
Midlife Crisis

Recreational Activities Dispute
Separation and Divorce
Work/Home Role Strain

Histrionic Personality Disorder
301.50
Communication
Infidelity
Intolerance
Personality Differences
Physical Abuse
Psychological Abuse

Hypoactive Sexual Desire Disorder
302.71
Infidelity
Sexual Abuse
Sexual Dysfunction

Intermittent Explosive Disorder
312.34
Blame
Sexual Abuse

Major Depressive Disorder   296.xx
Anger
Blame
Communication
Disillusionment with Relationship
Infidelity
Interventions with One Partner
Intolerance
Jealousy
Life-Changing Events
Loss of Love/Affection
Midlife Crisis
Physical Abuse
Psychological Abuse
Recreational Activities Dispute
Separation and Divorce

Major Depressive Episode   296.xx
Dependency
Depression Independent of
Relationship Problems
Depression Due to Relationship
Problems
Eating Disorder
Job Stress
Work/Home Role Strain

Male Erectile Disorder   **302.72**
Sexual Dysfunction

Male Hypoactive Sexual Desire
Disorder Due to Axis III Disorder
608.89
Sexual Dysfunction

Male Orgasmic Disorder   302.74
Sexual Abuse
Sexual Dysfunction

Narcissistic Personality Disorder
301.81
Anger
Blame
Communication
Financial Conflict
Infidelity
Interventions with One Partner
Intolerance
Jealousy
Personality Differences
Physical Abuse
Psychological Abuse
Separation and Divorce

Neglect of Child   **V61.21**
Parenting Conflicts—Adolescents
Parenting Conflicts—Children

Neglect of Child (995.52, Victim)
V61.21
Parenting Conflicts—Adolescents
Parenting Conflicts—Children

Obsessive-Compulsive Personality
Disorder   **301.4**
Financial Conflict
Intolerance
Personality Differences
Physical Abuse
Psychological Abuse

Occupational Problem   **V62.2**
Financial Conflict

Panic Disorder with Agoraphobia
300.21
Anxiety
Recreational Activities Dispute

Panic Disorder Without Agoraphobia   300.01
Anxiety

Paranoid Personality Disorder   301.0
Blame

Parent-Child Relational Problem   V61.20
Blended-Family Problems
Parenting Conflicts—Adolescents
Parenting Conflicts—Children

Partner Relational Problem   V61.1
Alcohol Abuse
Anger
Anxiety
Blame
Blended Family Problems
Communication
Depression Due to Relationship Problems
Disillusionment with Relationship
Eating Disorder
Financial Conflict
Infidelity
Interventions with One Partner
Intolerance
Jealousy
Life-Changing Events
Loss of Love/Affection
Midlife Crisis
Parenting Conflicts—Adolescents
Parenting Conflicts—Children
Personality Differences
Physical Abuse
Psychological Abuse
Recreational Activities Dispute
Religion/Spirituality Differences
Separation and Divorce

Physical Abuse of Adult (995.81, Victim)   V61.1
Anger
Communication
Depression Due to Relationship Problems
Interventions with One Partner
Intolerance
Jealousy

Loss of Love/Affection
Parenting Conflicts—Adolescents
Parenting Conflicts—Children
Physical Abuse
Psychological Abuse
Separation and Divorce

Physical Abuse of Child (995.5, Victim)   V61.21
Anger
Parenting Conflicts—Adolescents
Parenting Conflicts—Children

Physical Abuse of Partner (995.81, Victim)   V61.1
Sexual Abuse

Polysubstance Dependence   304.80
Eating Disorder

Posttraumatic Stress Disorder   309.81
Infidelity
Interventions with One Partner
Physical Abuse
Psychological Abuse

Premature Ejaculation   302.75
Sexual Dysfunction

Sexual Abuse of Child (995.5, Victim)   V61.21
Parenting Conflicts—Adolescents
Parenting Conflicts—Children
Sexual Dysfunction

Sexual Abuse of Partner (995.81, Victim)   V61.1
Sexual Abuse

Sexual Aversion Disorder   302.79
Sexual Abuse
Sexual Dysfunction

Sexual Disorder NOS   302.9
Sexual Abuse
Sexual Dysfunction

Sibling Relational Problem   V61.8
Blended-Family Problems

BIBLIOGRAPHY

American Psychiatric Association. (1994). *Diagnostic and statistical manual of mental disorders,* (4th ed.) Washington, DC: Author.

Barlow, D. H., & Craske, M. (1994) *Mastering your anxiety and panic—Patient's workbook.* San Antonio, TX: The Psychological Corporation.

Beattie, M. (1987). *Co-dependent no more: How to stop controlling others and start caring for yourself.* San Francisco: Harper.

Benedek, E. P., & Brown, C. F. (1995). *How to help your child overcome your divorce.* Washington, DC: American Psychiatric Press.

Burns, D. D. (1980). *Feeling good: The new mood therapy.* New York: Signet.

Comfort, A. (1991). *The new joy of sex.* New York: Crown.

Consumer Reports (January 1998).

Covey, Stephen. (1997). *The seven habits of highly effective families: Building a beautiful family culture in a turbulent world.* New York: Golden Books.

Craske, M., & Barlow, D. (1992) *Mastering your anxiety and worry—Patient's workbook.* San Antonio, TX: The Psychological Corporation.

Cummings, E. M., & Davies, P. (1994). *Children and marital conflict: The impact of family dispute and resolution.* New York: Guilford Press.

Dadds, M. R., Schwartz, S., & Saunders, M. R. (1987). Marital discord and treatment outcome in the treatment of childhood conduct disorders. *Journal of Consulting and Clinical Psychology, 55,* 396–403.

Evans, P. (1996). *The verbally abusive relationship: How to recognize it and how to respond.* Holbrook, MA: Adams.

Forgatch, M., & Patterson, G. R. (1987). *Parents and adolescents. Vol II: Family problem solving.* Eugene, OR: Castalia.

Friday, N. (1995). *My secret garden.* New York: Pocket.

Friday, N. (1993). *Women on top: How real life has changed women's sexual fantasies.* New York: Pocket.

Gardner, R. A. (1985). *The boys and girls book about divorce, with an introduction for parents.* New York: Bantam Books.

Gardner, R. A. (1991). *The parent's book about divorce.* New York: Bantam Books.

Greenberg, L. S., & Johnson, S. M. (1988). *Emotionally focused therapy for couples.* New York: Guilford Press.

Gurin, G., Veroff, J., & Feld, S. (1960). *Americans view their health: A nationwide interview survey.* New York: Basic Books.

Haley, J. (1987). *Problem-solving therapy* (2nd ed.). San Francisco: Jossey-Bass.

Heiman, J., & LoPiccolo, J. (1988). *Becoming orgasmic: A sexual growth program for women.* New York: Prentice-Hall.

Heyman, R. E., & Schlee, K. A. (in press). Stopping wife abuse via physical aggression couples treatment. In D. Dutton (Ed.), *Treatment of assaultiveness.* New York: Guilford Press.

Holmes, T. H., & Rahe, R. H. (1967). The social readjustment scale. *Journal of Psychosomatic Research, 11,* 213–218.

Jacobson, N. S., & Christensen, A. (1997). *Integrative couple therapy.* New York: Norton.

Johnson, V. (1980). *I'll quit tomorrow.* New York: Harper and Row.

Jongsma, A. E., & Peterson, L. M. (1995). *The complete psychotherapy treatment planner.* New York: Wiley.

Kaufman, T. S., & Coale, H. (1993). *The combined family: A guide to creating successful step-relationships.* New York: Plenum.

Kushner, H. S. (1997). *How good do we have to be?* New York: Little Brown.

McCarthy, B., & McCarthy, E. (1993). *Sexual Awareness: Enhancing Sexual Pleasure.* New York: Carroll & Graf.

McMahon, M., & Pence, E. (1996). Replying to Dan O'Leary. *Journal of interpersonal violence, 11,* 452–455.

Miller, W. R., & Muñoz, R. F. (1982). *How to control your drinking* (Rev. ed.). Albuquerque, NM: University of New Mexico Press.

National Institute on Alcohol Abuse and Alcoholism. (1996). *How to cut down on your drinking* (NIH pamphlet No. 96-3770). Available from NIAAA, P.O. Box 10686, Rockville, MD 20849-0686. (301) 443-3860. Web site: http://www.niaaa.nih.gov.

National Institute on Alcohol Abuse and Alcoholism. (1996). *Alcoholism: Getting the facts* (NIH Publication No. 96-4153). Available from NIAAA, P.O. Box 10686, Rockville, MD 20849-0686. (301) 443-3860. Web site: http://www.niaaa.nih.gov.

National Institute of Mental Health. (1994). *Eating disorders* (Brochure No. 94-3477). Available from NIMH Public Inquiries, 5600 Fishers Lane, Rm 7C-02, MSC 8030, Bethesda, MD 20892-8030. Web site: http://www.nimh.nih.gov/publist/puborder.htm.

Notarius, C., & Markman, H. (1993). *We can work it out.* New York: Putnam.

O'Farrell, T. J. (1993). *Treating alcohol problems: Marital and family interventions.* New York: Guilford Press.

O'Leary, K. D. (1996). Physical aggression in intimate relationships can be treated within a marital context under certain circumstances. *Journal of Interpersonal Violence, 11,* 450–452.

O'Leary, K. D., Christian, J. L., & Mendell, N. R. (1994). A closer look at the link between marital discord and depressive symptomatology. *Journal of Social and Clinical Psychology, 13,* 33–41.

Patterson, G. R., & Forgatch, M. (1987). *Parents and adolescents: Living together. Vol I: The basics.* Eugene, OR: Castalia.

Penner, C., & Penner, C. (1981). *The gift of sex.* Waco, TX: Word.

Pfiffner, L. J., Jouriles, E. N., Brown, M. M., Etscheid, M. A., & Kelly, J. A. (1990). Effects of problem solving training for single-parent families. *Journal of Family and Behavior Therapy, 12,* 1–11.

Pittman, F. (1990). *Private lies: Infidelity and betrayal of intimacy.* New York: Norton.

Prinz, R. J., Foster, S. L., Kent, R. N., & O'Leary, K. D. (1979). Multivariate assessment of conflict in distressed and nondistressed mother-adolescent dyads. *Journal of Applied Behavior Analysis, 12,* 691–700.

Prochaska, J. O., Velicer, W. F., Rossi, J. S., Goldstein, M. G., Marcus, B. H., Rakowski, W., Fiore, C., Harlow, L. L., Redding, C. A., Rosenbloom, D., & Rossi, S. R. (1994). Stages of change and decisional balance for 12 problem behaviors. *Health Psychology, 13,* 39–46.

Ricci, I. (1997). *Mom's house, dad's house: A complete guide for parents who are separated, divorced, or remarried.* New York: Fireside.

Robin, A. L., & Foster, S. L. (1989). *Negotiating parent-adolescent conflict.* New York: Guilford Press.

Robin, A. L., Koepke, T., & Moye, A. (1990). Multidimensional assessment of parent-adolescent relations. *Psychological Assessment, 2,* 451–459.

Roehling, P. V., & Robin, A. L. (1986). Development and validation of the family beliefs inventory: A measure of unrealistic beliefs among parents and adolescents. *Journal of Consulting and Clinical Psychology, 54,* 693–697.

Rosellini, G., & Worden, M. (1986). *Of course you're angry.* San Francisco: Harper Hazelden.

Rosenbaum, A., & O'Leary, K. D. (1986). Treatment of marital violence. In N. S. Jacobson & A. S. Gurman (Eds.), *Clinical handbook of marital therapy* (pp. 385–406). New York: Guilford Press.

Rubin, T. I. (1969). *The angry book.* New York: MacMillan.

Sanders, M. R. (1992). *Every parent: A positive approach to children's behavior.* Sydney: Addison-Wesley.

Sanders, M. R., & Dadds, M. R. (1993). *Behavioral family intervention.* Needham Heights, MA: Allyn & Bacon.

Sanders, M. R., Lynch, M. E., & Markie-Dadds, C. (1994). *Every parent's workbook: A positive guide to positive parenting.* Brisbane: Australian Academic Press.

Sanders, M. R., Markie-Dadds, C., & Nicholson, J. M. (1997). Concurrent interventions for marital and children's problems. In W. K. Halford & H. J. Markman (Eds.), *Clinical handbook of marriage and couples interventions.* New York: Wiley.

Smedes, L. (1991). *Forgive and forget: Healing the hurts we don't deserve.* San Francisco: Harper.

Spring, J. A. (1996). *After the affair: Healing the pain and rebuilding trust when a partner has been unfaithful.* New York: Harper Collins.

U.S. Department of Agriculture. *Family Economics Review,* published by the (Superintendent of Documents, U.S. Government Printing Office, Washington, DC 20402).

Valins, L. (1992). *When a woman's body says no to sex: Understanding and overcoming vaginismus.* New York: Penguin.

Veroff, J., Kulka, R. A., & Douvan, E. (1981). *Mental health in America: Patterns of help seeking from 1957 to 1976.* New York: Basic Books.

Vivian, D., & Heyman, R. E. (1996). Is there a place for conjoint treatment of couple violence? *In Session, 2,* 25–48.

Watzlawick, P., Weakland, J. H., & Fisch, R. (1974). *Change: Principles of problem formation and problem resolution.* New York: Norton.

Weissman, M. M. (1987). Advances in psychiatric epidemiology: Rate and risk for major depression. *American Journal of Public Health, 77,* 445–451.

Westheimer, R. (1995). *Sex for dummies.* New York: IDG Books.

Whisman, M. A., & Bruce, M. L. (1998). Marital distress and the incidence of major depressive episode in a community sample. Unpublished manuscript. Yale University, New Haven, CT.

Zilbergeld, B. (1992). *The new male sexuality.* New York: Bantam.

VIDEOS

Dodson, B. *Celebrating Orgasm: Women's Private Self-Loving Sessions.* Available from Tantra.com, P.O. Box 1818, Sebastopol, CA 95472. (800) 982-6872, or http://www.tantra.com.

Sinclair Institute. *Better sex videos: Volume 1: Better sexual techniques, Volume 2: Advanced sexual techniques, Volume 3: Making sex fun, Volume 8: You can last longer: Solutions for ejaculatory control.* Available from Sinclair Institute, P.O. Box 8865, Chapel Hill, NC 27515. (800) 955-0888, Ext. 8NET2, or http://www.bettersex.com.

Sinclair Institute. *Becoming orgasmic.* Video accompaniment to Heiman, J., & LoPiccolo, J. (1988). *Becoming orgasmic: A sexual growth program for women.* Available from Sinclair Institute, P.O. Box 8865, Chapel Hill, NC 27515. (800) 955-0888, Ext. 8NET2, or http://www.bettersex.com.

MEASURES

Adolescent Measures.

Issues Checklist (Foster & Robin, 1988); Conflict Behavior Questionnaire (Prinz, Foster, Kent, & O'Leary, 1979); Family Beliefs Inventory (Vincent, Roehling & Robin, 1986) Parent-Adolescent Relationship Questionnaire (Robin, Koepke, & Moye, 1986). See Robin, A. L., & Foster, S. L. (1989). *Negotiating parent-adolescent conflict.* New York: Guilford Press.

Areas of Change Questionnaire, Weiss & Birchler, 1975.
Available from Dr. Robert L. Weiss, Department of Psychology, University of Oregon, Eugene, OR 97403, or rlweiss@oregon.uoregon.edu.
Beck Depression Inventory.
Beck, A. T., Steer, R. A., & Garbin, M. G. (1988). Psychometric properties of the Beck Depression Inventory: Twenty-five years of evaluation. *Clinical Psychology Review, 8,* 77–100. Available from The Psychological Corporation, San Antonio, TX. (800) 228-0752.
Beck Hopelessness Inventory.
Available from The Psychological Corporation, San Antonio, TX. (800) 228-0752.
Child Behavior Checklist—Achenbach.
Achenbach, T., & Edelbrock, C. (1981). Behavior problems and competencies reported by parents of normal and disturbed children aged four through sixteen. *Monographs of the Society for Research in Child Development, 46,* (188).
Achenbach, T. M., Edelbrock, C., & Howell, C. T. (1987). Empirically based assessment of the behavior/emotional. Available from Dr. Achenbach at 1 South Prospect Street, The University of Vermont, Burlington, VT 05401-3456. (802) 656-8313, or checklist@uvm.edu.
Achenbach, T. M. (1991). *Integrative guide for the 1991 CBCL/4–18, YSR, and TRF profiles.* Burlington, VT: University of Vermont Department of Psychiatry.
Achenbach, T. M. (1992). *Manual for the child behavior checklist/2–3 and 1992 profile.* Burlington, VT: University of Vermont Department of Psychiatry.
Commitment Scale—Broderick & O'Leary.
Broderick, J., & O'Leary, K. D. (1986). Contributions of affect, attitudes and behavior to marital satisfaction. *Journal of Consulting and Clinical Psychology, 54,* 514–517.
Cost/Benefit Analysis, Birchler & Weiss, Weiss, 1977.
Available from Dr. Robert L. Weiss, Department of Psychology, University of Oregon, Eugene, OR 97403, or rlweiss@oregon.uoregon.edu.
Cost Benefit Analysis, Weiss, 1975.
Available from Dr. Robert L. Weiss, Department of Psychology, University of Oregon, Eugene, OR 97403, or rlweiss@oregon.uoregon.edu.
Inventory of Rewarding Activities, Birchler & Weiss, 1997.
Available from Dr. Robert L. Weiss, Department of Psychology, University of Oregon, Eugene, OR 97403, or rlweiss@oregon.uoregon.edu.
Locke Wallace Marital Adjustment Test.
Locke, H. J., & Wallace, K. M. (1959). Short marital adjustment and prediction tests: Their reliability and validity. *Marriage and Family Living, 21,* 251–255. Can be found in O'Leary, K. D. (1987). *Assessment of Marital Discord.* New York: Guilford.
Marital Satisfaction Inventory—Snyder.
Snyder, D. K. (1979). *Marital satisfaction inventory (MSI): Administration booklet.* Los Angeles: Western Psychological Services.

Marital Status Inventory—Weiss & Cerreto.
>Weiss, R. L., & Cerreto, M. C. (1980). The marital status inventory: Development of a measure of dissolution potential. *American Journal of Family Therapy, 8,* 80–86. Available from Dr. Robert L. Weiss, Department of Psychology, University of Oregon, Eugene, OR 97403, or rlweiss@oregon.uoregon.edu.

Parenting Scale—Arnold, O'Leary, Wolff, & Acker.
>Arnold, D. S., O'Leary, S. G., Wolff, L. S., & Acker, M. M. (1993). The parenting scale: A measure of dysfunctional parenting in discipline situations. *Psychological Assessment, 5,* 137–144.

Personal Assessment of Intimacy in Relationships (PAIR)—Olson.
>Schaefer, M. T., & Olson, David H. (1981). Assessing intimacy: The PAIR inventory. *Journal of Marital & Family Therapy, 7,* 47–60. Contact Life Innovations, Inc., P.O. Box 190, Minneapolis, MN 55440-0190. (612) 331-1661, or lifeinno@aol.com.

Positive Feelings Questionnaire.
>Can be found in O'Leary, K. D. (1987) *Assessment of Marital Discord.* New York: Guilford.

Relationship Satisfaction Questionnaire—Burns.
>Heyman, R. E., Sayers, S. L., & Bellack, A. S. (1994). Global marital satisfaction vs. marital adjustment: Construct validity and psychometric properties of three measures. *Journal of Family Psychology, 8,* 432–446. Available from Dr. David D. Burns, Department of Psychiatry, Presbyterian Medical Center of Philadelphia, 39th and Market Streets, Philadelphia, PA 19104.

Revised Conflict Tactics Scale—Straus.
>Straus, M. A., Hamby, S. L., Boney-McCoy, S., & Sugarman, D. B. (1996). The revised conflict tactics scales (CTS2): Development and preliminary psychometric data. *Journal of Family Issues, 17,* 283–316.

Sexual History Form—LoPiccolo.
>Can be found in O'Leary, K. D. (1987). *Assessment of marital discord.* New York: Guilford.

Spanier Dyadic Adjustment Scale.
>Spanier, G. B. (1976). Measuring dyadic adjustment: New scales for assessing the quality of marriage and similar dyads. *Journal of Marriage and the Family, 38,* 15–28.

Spouse Verbal Problem Checklist—Haynes.
>Haynes, S. N., Chavez, R. E., & Samuel, V. (1984). Assessment of marital communication and distress. *Behavioral Assessment, 6,* 315–322.

ABOUT THE DISK

TheraScribe® 3.0 Library Module Installation

The enclosed disk contains files to upgrade your TheraScribe® 3.0 program to include the behavioral definitions, goals, objectives, and interventions from *The Couples Psychotherapy Treatment Planner.*

Note: You must have TheraScribe® 3.0 for Windows installed on your computer in order to use *The Couples Psychotherapy Treatment Planner* library module.

To install the library module, please follow these steps:

1. Place the library module disk in your floppy drive.

2. Log in to TheraScribe® 3.0 as the Administrator using the name "Admin" and your administrator password.

3. On the Main Menu, press the "GoTo" button and choose the Options menu item.

4. Press the "Import Library" button.

5. On the Import Library Module screen, choose your floppy disk drive a:\ from the list and press "Go". Note: It may take a few minutes to import the data from the floppy disk to your computer's hard disk.

6. When the installation is complete the library module data will be available in your TheraScribe® 3.0 program.

Note: If you have a network version of TheraScribe® 3.0 installed, you should import the library module one time only. After importing the data, the library module data will be available to all network users.

User Assistance

If you need assistance using this TheraScribe® 3.0 add-on module, call Wiley Technical Support at (212) 850-6753, weekdays beween 9 AM and 4 PM Eastern Standard Time. You can also email Wiley Technical Support at techhelp@wiley.com.

For information on how to install disk, refer to the **About the Disk** section on page 265.

WILEY
Publishers Since 1807